THE LOSS OF
The Bismarck

D1571565

THE LOSS OF
The Bismarck

Vice-Admiral B. B. SCHOFIELD CB, CBE

*This book is published and distributed
in the United States by the*

UNITED STATES NAVAL INSTITUTE

Annapolis, Maryland 21402

First published in 1972

SBN 7110 0265 7

Published by Ian Allan Ltd, Shepperton, Surrey
and printed in the United Kingdom by
Morrison and Gibb Ltd, London and Edinburgh

Contents

42467

DIAGRAMS

Acknowledgements

My thanks are due to all those who in one way or another have
assisted me in the preparation of this book, in particular to the
Librarians and staffs of the Admiralty, Imperial War Museum, and
Royal United Service Institute's Libraries; to Dr Jürgen Rohwer of
the Bibliothek für Zeitgeschicte, Stuttgart, for permission to make use
of the sketches of the *Bismarck*'s movements which he prepared for
the late Captain Gerhard Bidlingmaier's study *Erfolg und Ende des
Schlachtschiffes Bismarck* and published in Wehrwissenschaftliche
Umschau, Heft 5/59 as well as in Herr Brennecke's book, *Schlachtschiff Bismarck*; and to Mrs Erika Gillett for her translations. The
photographs reproduced are by the courtesy of the Imperial War
Museum.

B. B. Schofield, *May 1971*

Holme,
Lower Shiplake

Introduction

In 1867 an unknown Captain in the Royal Marine Artillery, John Charles Ready Colomb published anonymously a small book entitled *The Protection of our Commerce and Distribution of Naval Forces considered*. Already at that time the need to import food to feed a growing population of 26 millions, and raw materials to supply a rapidly expanding industry, made it clear that Britain was very vulnerable to any interference with her sea communications, but it took a long time for this fact to be appreciated by those responsible for the country's defence. Colomb died in 1909, having spent his life in preaching what was ultimately proved to be a thoroughly sound naval strategy, but by and large his views were not given much attention. As events moved towards the outbreak of World War I, interest was concentrated on the possible outcome of a clash between the battlefleets which Britain and Germany had been building in intense competition with each other during the previous decade. Yet when war came, it was the threat to her sea communications offered by the German U-boats which brought Britain to the brink of defeat.

In the inter-war years, treaties, pacts and negotiations were the order of the day and under the Geneva Convention Britain sought to obtain immunity from submarine attack for her shipping on which she was now more than ever dependent, the population having reached 46 millions by 1931. Further, the use of indigenous coal was being extensively replaced by imported oil in industry, and in the Royal Navy wholly so. Fortunately, as the threat of another war with Germany loomed larger, the Admiralty rightly suspecting that the Geneva Convention prohibiting attacks on merchant ships without making provision for the safety of their crews, to which Germany had subscribed, would not be observed once hostilities began, made arrangements to institute convoy in the North Atlantic. It soon became apparent that the forces available were totally insufficient to provide protection on the scale required, but it was the agreed opinion that a lightly escorted convoy was better than independent sailing. This time there were no opposing battlefleets, and from the outset Germany concentrated her attacks on British sea communications, although her navy too was lacking in the means to do so as effectively as it would have liked. Nevertheless, the best use was made of the forces available, and by the end of 1939 after only four months of war, they had accounted for over $\frac{3}{4}$ million tons of shipping. The following year, 1940, which saw the German occupation of Norway and Denmark, followed soon after by that of Holland, Belgium and the greater part of France, the toll grew alarmingly to reach almost four million tons. But in the face of all these disasters, under Winston Churchill's forceful leadership, and with the generous help of the United States, Britain was striving to build up her ability to continue the war alone. In factories throughout the land the highest priority was being given to war production, but the inescapable fact remained that, without a steady flow of raw materials, food, arms and equipment from North America and the Empire, all these efforts would be in vain. Germany now controlled the Atlantic coast of Europe from the North Cape to the Spanish frontier and this had greatly advantaged her in the conduct of the war against shipping which her U-boats were waging in the Atlantic. These, with some help from long-range Focke Wulf aircraft operating from ports and airfields in occupied France, were taking an increasing toll of British and Allied merchant vessels. Mr Churchill has recorded his anxiety at that time:

'How much would the U-boat warfare reduce our imports and shipping? Would it ever reach the point where our life would be destroyed? Here was no field for gestures or sensations; only the slow, cold drawing of lines on charts, which showed potential strangulation. Compared with this there was no value in brave armies ready to leap upon the invader, or in a good plan for desert warfare. The high and faithful spirit of the people counted for nought in this bleak domain. Either the food, supplies and arms from the New World and from the British Empire arrived across the oceans or they failed.'*

* *The Second World War*, Winston Churchill, Vol. II, p. 529, Cassell and Company.

And there was good reason for the Prime Minister's uneasiness. At the end of January the German battle-cruisers *Scharnhorst* and *Gneisenau* had succeeded in breaking out into the Atlantic where they had sunk or captured twenty-two ships totalling 115000 tons and early in February the heavy cruiser *Hipper*, on a second foray into the Atlantic, had sunk seven ships totalling 32806 tons, out of a nineteen-ship homewardbound convoy from Sierra Leone. In the first three months of 1941 raiders accounted for 37 ships totalling 187662 tons and this added to the toll taken by the U-boats and other causes accounted for almost one and a half million tons of shipping. These activities were placing an ever-increasing strain on the limited resources of the Royal Navy, because to locate a skilfully handled raider in the vastness of the oceans required, as had already been found, a large number of ships and aircraft, and the last named especially were in very short supply.

German Strength and Weakness

Grand Admiral Erich Raeder, Commander-in-Chief of the German navy was a man of great experience and determination. During World War I he had been Chief of Staff to Admiral Franz von Hipper, Commander of the First Scouting Group and Beatty's redoubtable opponent in the clash between the opposing battle-cruisers at the battle of Jutland. During that war the German High Seas fleet had spent much of its time in harbour and afterwards there was a great deal of criticism to the effect that its offensive value had not been as fully exploited as it should have been. He was determined not to repeat the mistakes of his predecessors Admirals von Pohl and Scheer and from the outset had determined on an offensive policy, despite the inferiority of his fleet *vis-à-vis* that of the British, and so far it had met with considerable success. The damage inflicted on British shipping by the pocket battleships in the first months of the war, despite the unnecessary loss of the *Graf Spee*; the risks taken during the Norwegian campaign, which notwithstanding heavy losses had paid a handsome dividend; the success of the two battle-cruisers during their recent sortie into the Atlantic; all these encouraged him in the belief that, 'offence is still the best means of defence'. He knew too that if Britain's lifeline with North America and other overseas sources of supply could be severed, she would not be able to continue the war. He did not, however, yet possess an adequate number of submarines to bring this about, and the effect of the sorties by the pocket battleships, cruisers and battle-cruisers already mentioned had been to oblige the British to use their battleships as escorts to their North Atlantic convoys. This policy had prevented the German surface ships from attacking such convoys and therefore from sinking as many ships as they might otherwise have done, but at last he saw a way of achieving what he hoped might prove a decisive blow. The new battleship *Bismarck* was now operational, and he well knew that she was superior in every way to any similar class of ship in the British navy. But for all what he calls, 'her unusually powerful fighting strength' Raeder was worried by his inability to provide his ships with air cover and this he fully appreciated was 'a weak point in our armour' and one about which he could do nothing since the war having broken out earlier than he had been led to expect, he had not had time to complete the building of any carriers. However, for the reasons given above, he decided to ignore this weakness, but he could have wished that his opposite number, the Commander-in-Chief of the German Air Force, Reichsmarshal Herman Göring would be more co-operative, for there was quite a lot that shore-based aircraft could do to make up for the lack of a naval air arm.

The Bismarck
The battleship *Bismarck* was the fourth ship to bear the name of the 'blood and iron' Chancellor who, paradoxically, though he had forged the unity of the German nation, had seen no need for it to possess a navy. Since her commissioning on April 24, 1940, she had been in the Baltic overcoming the teething troubles found in all new ships, and working her crew up to the highest pitch of efficiency. When at the end of November 1938 Raeder had shown Hitler the designs of the two new powerful battleships, the keels of which had been laid two years previously, the latter had criticised them, 'declaring that they were insufficiently gunned and too slow', but the Grand Admiral knew better. Officially stated to conform to the 1922 Washington Treaty limit of 35000 tons, the *Bismarck* and her sister ship the *Tirpitz* had a maximum displacement of 50900 tons and 52600 tons respectively, a secret which had been very well kept. Great attention had been paid to their underwater protection which, in addition to bulkheads of unusual strength, comprised a large number of compartments or cells capable of absorbing water pressure and of allowing the upward venting of the force of an explosion. These anti-torpedo compartments were constructed of a special

kind of steel of great toughness and elasticity, capable of being bent by the force of an explosion without cracking. They were sited immediately below the armoured belt and within the hull plating. As regards armour, a $12\frac{1}{2}$in (32cm) belt of the best hardened Krupp steel, 170m long covered the vital parts of the ship and extended from 3m above to 2m below the water line; although not proof against a direct hit by a 15in (380mm) shell, it was believed that any engagement with a similarly armed ship would be fought at a range which would ensure only a glancing impact, which such high quality steel would be able to withstand. The horizontal armour comprised an upper deck made from 2in (5cm) special steel designed to detonate the fuses of shell and bombs before they were able to penetrate to vital parts of the ship. Below this was a main deck covering four-fifths of the ship's length made from armour plate 4in (12cm) thick, with sloping sides $4\frac{3}{4}$in (12cm) thick, reaching down almost to the lower edge of the side armour. It was claimed, with some justification and borne out by subsequent events, that these ships were virtually unsinkable. Originally designed to be powered by diesel engines so as to give them a very long endurance, the need to accelerate their construction led to the substitution of high pressure Wagner type boilers feeding three sets of turbines driving three propellers to give a designed speed of 29 knots. On trials the *Bismarck* reached 30·8 knots. This then, was the ship upon which Raeder pinned his hopes.

The Prinz Eugen

The heavy cruiser *Prinz Eugen*, detailed to accompany the *Bismarck* on her sortie into the Atlantic, was a sister ship of the *Hipper* and the unlucky *Blücher*, sunk during the invasion of Norway. They were officially supposed to conform to the 10000 tons limit for cruisers laid down under the 1922 Washington Treaty, but in fact their tonnage was nearly double that amount, being 18500 tons at deep load. In speed and protection they outclassed the 8in gun cruisers in the British fleet. She was the first ship in the German navy to bear the name, her immediate predecessor being the 20000 ton battleship of the Austrian navy in World War I which in turn had been named after the French General François Eugene, Prince of Savoy, and ally of Churchill's ancestor the Duke of Marlborough at the battle of Blenheim. In addition to a main armament of eight 8in (203mm) guns she carried twelve 4·1in (104mm) A/A guns and twelve torpedoes. She became known in the German navy as 'the lucky ship'.

Operation Rheinübung (Rhine Exercise)

Raeder's plan to which the code name of Operation 'Rheinübung' was given, involved a simultaneous sortie into the Atlantic by the battleship *Bismarck* and the cruiser *Prinz Eugen* from the Baltic, and the battle-cruisers *Scharnhorst* and *Gneisenau* from Brest. to which port they had returned after their last sortie. The ships were to rendezvous at a pre-arranged position, and with this powerful force he was confident that any convoy encountered could be over-whelmed. A series of such disasters would, he was sure, lead to a suspension of sailings and moreover such a concentration would pose a very difficult problem for the British who might be obliged to withdraw their battleships from the Mediterranean to meet it, and thus facilitate the domination of that area by the Italian fleet. Arrangements had been made to support the ships with five tankers and two supply ships, and special reconnaissance would be provided by U-boats and disguised merchantmen. It was a bold, imaginative plan, typical of the man who made it, and might well have succeeded, but for a series of unforseen incidents.

Originally timed to be put into operation during the new moon period at the end of April, the first setback occurred when it was discovered that there would be a delay in the completion of the *Scharnhorst*'s refit at Brest. Then on April 6 an aircraft from Coastal Command of the Royal Air Force torpedoed the *Gneisenau* as she lay at anchor there, and five days later, after she had been moved into dry dock she was severely damaged during a raid on the port by aircraft from Bomber Command. Later as a result of running over a ground mine laid by aircraft in the Baltic, the *Prinz Eugen* suffered damage to a coupling, necessitating a postponement to the latter part of May when the moon would again be new.

Raeder had selected to command the operation an admiral in whom, he has recorded, he had the greatest confidence, the fifty-two year old Günther Lütjens who had served with distinction in Torpedo boats during World War I. The outbreak of World War II found him in command of all destroyers and fast patrol boats. In March 1940, as a temporary relief for Admiral Wilhelm Marschal who had gone sick, he commanded the battle-cruisers *Scharnhorst* and *Gneisenau* during the Norwegian campaign and in July he was confirmed in the appointment. He had recently returned from a successful foray with these ships into the Atlantic. He has been described as, 'one of Germany's ablest officers since the first World War. Very deliberate and intelligent, level-headed in his judgment of situations and people; incorruptible in his views, unassuming and an engaging person when you knew him well; devoid of vanity and without overweening ambition. His dry humour made him well liked amongst his comrades'.*

When Raeder informed Lütjens of his decision to mount the operation the latter pointed out that it would be far more effective if it were postponed until either the battle-cruisers or the *Tirpitz* were ready for sea. He also suggested that the appearance of the *Bismarck* in the Atlantic would cause the British Admiralty to take measures which would jeopardise the chances of success for an operation in strength at a later date with the other ships. While fully agreeing with him on this point, Raeder was obviously not prepared to change his views, for he went on to caution him about using Brest for the shortest possible time and only to replenish with ammunition or because of heavy damage. He ended, 'It is advisable to operate with caution. It is wrong to play for high stakes for a limited, possibly uncertain success. Our aim must be to carry out continuous operations with the *Bismarck* and later with the *Tirpitz* as well. To seek out a fight is not an end in itself, but only a means towards achieving the object which is to sink enemy tonnage. As long as this can be achieved without high stakes, so much the better'.† In his book Raeder says he was concerned at, 'the gradual improvement of the enemy's countermeasures and in particular at the strengthening of his air reconnaissance system'.‡

So all things considered, he decided that the operation must be carried out by the *Bismarck* and *Prinz Eugen* alone, as soon as repairs to the last-named were completed. The date finally selected was May 18.

It was a comparatively minor operation for the Commander-in-Chief of the sea-going forces to command in person, a point of view which Admiral Conrad Patzig put to Lütjens when they were discussing the operation a week before it was due to begin, but while

* Schlachtschiff *Bismarck*, by J. Brennecke, p. 259. (In a letter to the author from Admiral Patzig.)
† Brennecke, *ibid.*, p. 43.
‡ Raeder, *ibid.*, p. 212.

agreeing, Lütjens had no desire to query Raeder's decision though he appears to have had some premonition of the outcome, for he ended the interview by saying, 'I shall have to sacrifice myself sooner or later. I have renounced my private life and I am determined to execute the task which has been entrusted to me in an honourable manner'.*

Although there is no record in the Führer Naval Conferences that Hitler's approval was sought to the launching of operation 'Rhein-übung' and Raeder says categorically, 'The responsibility for sending out the *Bismarck* was mine,'† we have it on the authority of Captain (later Admiral) Puttkamer, Hitler's adjutant, that at the eleventh hour the Führer attempted to intervene. While the *Bismarck* was at Gotthafen she was visited by Hitler, but Raeder being absent, the question of her employment was not discussed. It was not until the Grand Admiral appeared at the Berghof on May 22 and mentioned, almost casually, that the ships had sailed, that Hitler enquired what they were doing. On being told he, 'expressed lively misgivings' and wanted them to be recalled. He was worried about the reactions of the United States, the possible complications with the launching of operation Barbarossa (the invasion of Russia planned to begin on June 1), and finally the risks of attacks on them by British aircraft carriers. Only after considerable discussion did Hitler agree to their proceeding as planned.‡

* Brennecke, *ibid.*, p. 50.
† Raeder, *ibid.*, p. 212.
‡ Brennecke, *ibid.*, p. 71.

destroyers (*Electra*, *Echo*, *Anthony*, *Icarus*, *Achates* and *Antelope*) to leave Scapa and proceed to Hvalfiord, Iceland, so as to be in a position to support the cruisers patrolling the straits on either side of Iceland. The ships sailed at midnight. At dawn the next day six Whitley and six Hudson aircraft of Coastal Command attacked the German ships as they lay at anchor. The weather conditions were bad and the visibility poor, so that only two aircraft reached the fiord, and they dropped their loads of armour-piercing bombs on the off-chance of a hit, but without success.

Throughout the day, despite steadily deteriorating weather conditions, reconnaissance was maintained off the Norwegian coast and in order to do so, every available aircraft in the northeast area was pressed into service. However, the visibility was so poor that they were unable to see whether the ships were still in the fiord or not. An attempt made that night by eighteen aircraft of the Royal Air Force Bomber Command to attack the German ships also failed; the coast was shrouded in fog and only two aircraft succeeded in reaching the target area, but were unable to identify anything. The German ships had in fact, sailed shortly before the abortive attack took place and the flash of the bursting bombs led Admiral Lütjens to believe that his departure had not been noticed.

CHAPTER TWO

British Home Fleet Sails

Admiral Tovey was anxiously awaiting further news of the enemy ships but, as has been mentioned, air reconnaissance proved useless in the prevailing weather. The Germans were similarly handicapped in obtaining information about the movements of British ships and a pilot who flew over Scapa Flow that day failed to notice the departure of the *Hood* and *Prince of Wales*, and belief that they were still in harbour reinforced Lütjen's opinion that he had made an unobserved departure. When, almost twenty-four hours had elapsed since the last sighting of the German ships, the Commanding Officer of the Royal Naval Air Station at Hatston in the Orkneys, Captain H. St. J. Fancourt RN ordered a twin-engined Maryland aircraft normally used for height-finding exercises to be got ready. It was manned by Lieutenant-Commander (A) N. E. Goddard RNVR as pilot, Commander G. A. Rotherham RN as observer, and a radio operator and rear gunner chosen from a large number of volunteers. Although time was of the essence, it was most important to prepare the flight plan carefully to decide where on the Norwegian coast to make a landfall, and at what height to approach in order to avoid interception by the enemy's radar and by his fighters of which large numbers were believed to be stationed in that area. By 1600 all was ready and half an hour later the aircraft took off and succeeded in reaching the coast in fair visibility. An examination of Korsfiord showed that the anchorage was empty and after a look at Bergen where heavy A/A fire was encountered the news of the enemy's departure was signalled and reached Admiral Tovey at 1900. It was confirmed after the aircraft landed in the Shetlands at 1915. The Commander-in-Chief immediately gave orders for the ships remaining in Scapa to prepare for sea and to be ready to sail at 2200. He signalled Vice-Admiral Holland not to call at Hvalfiord with his force, but to take up a position covering the patrols in the Denmark Straits and Iceland–Faroes passage, operating north of 62°N. He ordered the *Suffolk* to join the *Norfolk* on patrol, timing her departure so as to arrive in the Denmark Straits at the earliest time the *Bismarck* could arrive there in order to conserve fuel. The *Arethusa* was to support the *Manchester* and *Birmingham* in the Iceland–Faroes passage. Finally he ordered the battle-cruiser *Repulse* to join him off the Butt of Lewis at 0700 the following morning.

At 2300 Admiral Tovey in his flagship the *King George V* accompanied by the cruisers *Galatea*, *Aurora*, *Kenya*, *Hermione*, and the destroyers *Inglefield* (Captain D.), *Intrepid*, *Active*, *Punjabi*, *Nestor*, *Windsor* and *Lance* headed west from Scapa through the Pentland Firth. The *Lance* soon had to return on account of boiler trouble.

German Operation Orders

Admiral Lütjens' orders were clear. He was to attack enemy supply traffic in the Atlantic north of the Equator. The duration of the operation was left to his discretion. He was to proceed into the Atlantic via the Great Belt, the Skaggerak and the Norwegian Sea and was to attempt to break through unobserved. Even if the break-out were observed, the mission as defined above remained unaltered, but he was to avoid taking risks which might jeopardise the success of the operation and should avoid encounters with ships of superior or equal strength. If, however, such an encounter proved inevitable, then it should be an all-out (Ger. unter vollen Einsatz) engagement. These instructions differed in one important respect from those he had received when in command of the battle-cruisers for their earlier sortie—they permitted attacks on escorted convoys unless these were escorted by a group of ships which together could be considered superior to the *Bismarck*. The Admiral was warned that the lightness of the nights would add to the difficulty of making an unobserved break-out, but that poor visibility to be expected along the ice edge in the Denmark Straits would be a factor in his favour, and although enemy patrols might be encountered in both the Iceland–Faroes passage and the Denmark Straits, the indications were that they were not yet equipped with radar.

Movements of the Bismarck and Prinz Eugen

The *Bismarck* and *Prinz Eugen* left Gdynia on the evening of May 18 escorted by minesweepers, aircraft and U-boats, made an uneventful passage through the Great Belt and Skagerrak and reached Kristiansand South on the evening of May 20. Photographic reconnaissance of Scapa Flow showed that the Home Fleet was in harbour and air reconnaissance of the Denmark Straits, though hindered by bad weather, indicated that the ice edge lay between seventy and eighty miles from the North Cape (Iceland) thus giving a clear passage of twenty to thirty miles between it and the edge of the British mine-field. At 0900 on May 21 the two ships entered Korsfiord near Bergen where they refuelled and where, as already mentioned, they were sighted by a British reconnaissance aircraft. The ships themselves did not observe this aircraft and it was only from a British message intercepted by the monitoring service that forenoon that the German Naval Staff learned that the movement of the ships had become known to the British. Leaving Korsfiord at 2300 with an escort of three destroyers, which were detached off Trondheim, they continued northward until reaching latitude 65° 30′N when course was altered to the westward to pass north of Iceland with the intention of reaching the entrance to the Denmark Straits at about 0700 on May 23. Although he had been informed that the presence of his ships in Korsfiord had become known to the enemy, Admiral Lütjens was optimistic about his chances of slipping through the British patrol line, as his meteorological officer had forecast fog which was just what he wanted. He had decided on using the Denmark Straits against the advice of Group North because he hoped it would afford him better chances of concealment, and so while Raeder was pleading with Hitler not to recall them, through the night of May 22/23 the two darkened ships headed west at 25 knots.

Interception

For Admiral Tovey the situation was full of uncertainty which increased with every hour that passed without further news of the enemy ships. The weather was still preventing reconnaissance of the Norwegian coast but during daylight Sunderland flying boats and Hudson aircraft were keeping a constant watch over the passages between Iceland and the Faroes and also between the last-named and the Shetlands, despite strong head winds, rain squalls, heavy cloud and fog patches. Two Catalina flying boats despatched to cover the Denmark Straits were obliged to return owing to continuous heavy rain and thick cloud down to a height of 300 feet.

As soon as the *Repulse* screened by the destroyers *Legion*, *Saguenay* and *Assiniboine* joined his force at 0710 on 23rd the Commander-in-Chief altered the course of his force to northwest so as to take up a position covering the southern approach to the Faroes–Iceland passage. He had now disposed his fleet so as to cover both the possible channels by which the enemy might attempt to break out into the Atlantic, but as he had no information as to the time of his departure from Korsfiord, the possible area in which he might be, already large, was getting more so with every hour that passed. Weather again prevented air reconnaissance and in the prevailing poor visibility and with the limited forces available for patrolling, the chances of interception were anything but good. It was always possible that the enemy, acting on the assumption that his departure had been observed, might be waiting somewhere north of the Arctic Circle until he reckoned that some of the ships waiting to intercept him had to return to harbour to refuel. This possibility was very much to the fore in Admiral Tovey's mind.

When on May 23 the *Suffolk* joined his flag, Rear-Admiral

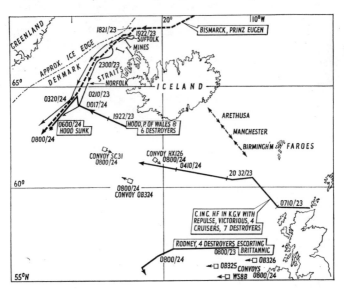

Diagram 1. Operation
'Rheinübung', May 23, 1941.
The sighting of the *Bismarck*.

Wake-Walker instructed her to investigate the ice edge up to the minefield and then to patrol within radar range of the former in a north-easterly and south-westerly direction on a three hour beat, so as to be at the southern end at 2200 and every six hours thereafter. If the weather remained clear towards the land the *Norfolk* would keep fifteen miles to the east of her but if it thickened and she had to close the shore, the two ships were to rendezvous in a specified position at 1300 the following day to co-ordinate their movements. In fact the weather conditions in the Denmark Straits on the afternoon of the 23rd were unusual. It was clear over the ice pack and some ten miles of water adjoining it, but the rest of the Straits as far as the Iceland coast was covered in thick mist. Because of this, the *Suffolk* on reaching the top of the minefield, steamed further to the east than would otherwise have been prudent, and kept close to the edge of the mist to have cover handy in case of need.

At noon on that day the *Bismarck* and *Prinz Eugen* began the most risky part of their voyage as they shaped course to pass between the ice edge and the minefield off the northwest coast of Iceland. The weather described above was not at all what Admiral Lütjens had been led to expect. At 1900 the two ships reached the narrowest part of the channel and may well have begun to feel that luck was on their side, but twenty-two minutes later, a lookout covering the stern sector in the *Suffolk*, which had just turned to the southwest after investigating the ice edge, reported two ships bearing 020° 7 miles. A quick look through binoculars confirmed the presence of the *Bismarck* and another similar looking vessel steering to the southwest. Captain R. M. Ellis RN commanding the *Suffolk*, immediately increased to full speed and turned his ship towards a gap in the minefield and took cover in the mist until the enemy ships had passed, at the same time sending out an enemy report.

Force H Ordered to Sail

The news that the two enemy ships had been sighted heading for the Atlantic increased the Admiralty's concern for the safety of the eleven British convoys at sea there, which included the troop convoy of five ships designated WS.8B which had left the Clyde on May 21 and which the *Victorious* and *Repulse* were to have escorted during its passage to the Middle East. It now had only an escort of two cruisers and eight destroyers. At 0500/24 a signal was therefore sent to Vice-Admiral Sir James Somerville, flag officer commanding Force H based on Gibraltar, to sail and steer to the northward to cover this convoy. Force H comprised the modernised battle-cruiser HMS *Renown* (flagship), the carrier HMS *Ark Royal*, the 6in gun cruiser HMS *Sheffield* and the destroyers *Faulknor, Foresight, Forester, Fox-hound, Fury* and *Hesperus*. Although the *Renown* was no match for the *Bismarck*, this force was destined to play a significant part.

Shadowing Tactics

When Coastal Command received news of the sighting of the German ships, a Sunderland flying boat and a Hudson reconnaissance aircraft were sent from Iceland to assist in maintaining touch with the enemy. The Hudson failed to find them and returned, but the flying boat held on throughout the night though it did not make contact with the *Suffolk* until the following morning. The cruiser had recently been fitted with Type 284 Radar (see Appendix II) which although trainable, had a blind spot over the stern, otherwise she would probably have located the *Bismarck* earlier than she did. As soon as the enemy ships had drawn ahead and were on a forward bearing, Captain Ellis took up a position for shadowing them. An hour later he was joined by the *Norfolk* which at the time of the sighting was some 15 miles away to the southwest. The cruiser flagship was equipped with radar Type 286P which had two fixed aerials and so could only take ranges on an ahead bearing. In closing in she was less fortunate than her consort. The *Bismarck* had by now picked up the pulses of the *Suffolk*'s radar transmissions and was on the alert. At 2030 when the *Norfolk* appeared out of the mist at a range of about six miles, she was greeted with five salvoes from the battleship's main armament and obliged to beat a hasty retreat. Fortunately she was not hit and sent out an enemy report timed 2032/23. The enemy ships were hugging the ice edge and thus forcing the *Suffolk* to keep more or less astern of them, so the *Norfolk* took up position on their port quarter, relying on a plot of the *Suffolk*'s regular reports to warn her of any sudden change in the enemy's course and/or speed. Although the German ships were fitted with search radar known as DT equipment, they did not have an accurate gunnery set and so were unable to drive off the shadowers using radar controlled blind fire. On discovering that his ships had been sighted, Admiral Lütjens increased their speed to 28 knots in the hope presumably of outdistancing his pursuers and he ordered the *Prinz Eugen* to take station ahead of the *Bismarck* and so clear the range for the latter's after guns should the shadowers approach too close. The German report of the operation refers to the surprise occasioned by the discovery that the British ships were equipped with, 'excellently functioning radar equipment' which it is claimed was 'of decisive importance for the further course of the operation' and which deprived them of the advantage to be gained from poor visibility.

Although the Admiralty picked up the *Suffolk*'s enemy report Admiral Tovey remained in ignorance of the event until he received the *Norfolk*'s report timed 2032. Vice-Admiral Holland, however, had received one of the *Suffolk*'s reports timed 1939 and it showed the enemy ships to be about 300 miles to the northward of him, bearing 005°. He was thus very favourably placed to cut them off if they continued on a south-westerly course. At 2054 therefore he ordered his force to increase speed to 27 knots and to steer a course of 295° which he estimated would enable him to make contact with them during the early hours of May 24. The steady flow of reports coming in from the shadowing cruisers enabled an accurate plot to be kept of the enemy's movements and minor adjustments to be made to bring about an encounter at a time and on a bearing favourable to the British ships. So far as the *Hood* was concerned it was imperative to close as quickly as possible to a range at which the trajectory of the enemy's 15in shell would be more nearly horizontal, ie about 12000 yards, because of the known weakness of that ship's horizontal armour. The *Prince of Wales*, on the other hand, not only had a 15in armoured belt but a 6in armoured deck and was considered safe from vital hits down to a range of about 13000 yards. It was difficult to reconcile the conflicting claims of an old battle-cruiser and a new battleship, but on balance the Admiral decided on an approach from fine on the *Bismarck*'s bow which would give a high closing rate and enable the action to be fought at a comparatively short range. Just before midnight the cruiser's shadowing reports suddenly ceased. A snowstorm had enveloped the German ships and their shadowers. It caused considerable clutter on the radar screens and in the semi-twilight of an arctic night in May produced some strange mirage effects. The cruiser captains were aware that the enemy might at any time decide to reverse his course and that if they failed to react promptly to such a move they would be blown out of the water by his big guns. When therefore the lookouts in the *Suffolk* saw what looked like the dark shadow of a ship bearing down on them Captain Ellis immediately put his helm hard over and turned to a reciprocal course. When he realised that he had been deceived and turned back to resume the chase, he had dropped so far astern that radar contact had been lost. It took him three hours to regain it. The *Norfolk* too lost touch and the sudden cessation of information appears to have led Vice-Admiral Holland to assume that the enemy ships had taken drastic action to throw off their shadowers either by a reversal of course to re-enter the Denmark Straits or by a major alteration to the south or southeast. At 2359 therefore, he ordered his force to steer north and to reduce speed to 25 knots. What his exact motives were in making this turn will never be known. There is some support for the belief that he may have been contemplating a night action because at 0015 he signalled that contact with the enemy might be expected any time after 0140/24 and ordered his ships to prepare for action. He must, however, have been aware that if the enemy ships were continuing along their last reported course and at the same speed, he was placing himself in a position of tactical disadvantage by allowing them to gain so much bearing knowing that his ships did not have a sufficient margin of speed to regain it. It is also possible, of course, that the plot in the *Hood* showed the *Bismarck* to be further off and more to the eastward than she was, since at that time there was no opportunity of co-ordinating positions with *Norfolk* and *Suffolk*.

At 0031 Admiral Holland informed his force that if the enemy ships had not been sighted by 0210 he would probably alter course to the southward (180°) until the cruisers regained touch, and also that he intended both ships to engage the *Bismarck*, leaving the *Prinz Eugen* to the two cruisers. However, Admiral Wake-Walker was not informed of the part he was expected to play in the forth-coming action; in fact his first intimation of the presence of Admiral Holland's force in his vicinity was when at 0445 he intercepted a message from the destroyer *Icarus* giving her position and that of the *Achates*, which showed them to be some distance astern of the *Norfolk*. At 0147 Admiral Holland told his destroyers to continue to search to the northward should the battle-cruisers (*sic*) alter course to 200° at 0205. There were now only four of them, the *Anthony* and *Antelope* having been detached at 1400/23 to fuel in Iceland.

At 0203, as the brief arctic night was beginning to lift, no further news having been received of the enemy, the force altered course to 200°, approximately parallel to the enemy's last reported course. At the same time the Admiral told the *Prince of Wales* to use her gunnery radar Type 284, to search for the enemy, who unknown to him was at that time 35 miles away to the northwest. When Captain Leach asked permission to use his search radar Type 281 instead as the gunnery set would not bear right aft, permission was refused for reasons it is difficult to conjecture. It may have been because all-round search of Type 281 was more liable to interception and direction finding than the more directional beam of Type 284. Also this latter set worked on 50cm wave length and a much higher frequency than any set used by the Germans at that time.

As suddenly as she had lost it, the *Suffolk* regained contact with the *Bismarck* at 0247 and again began to transmit a series of shadowing reports. These together with Direction Finding bearings of the cruisers taken by the *Prince of Wales* must have enabled the *Hood* to make an accurate assessment of the enemy's ship's position, course and speed which would have shown that they were still steering south-southwest at 28 knots. This must have made it plain to Admiral Holland, if he was not already aware of it, that he had lost so much bearing on the enemy that an end on approach was now impossible. Matters were made even worse when at 0320, Admiral Lütjens, in conformity with his policy of hugging the ice edge, altered course to the westward (230°) thereby putting the British force only fifteen degrees before his beam, distant 25 miles, though at this stage he was still unaware of its presence. Had Admiral Holland been forty or fifty miles ahead of his opponent, this unexpected move on the enemy's part could perhaps have been allowed for, but now it was too late, especially as it apparently took some time for it to be noticed. It was not until 0340 that he altered the course of his force to 240° to conform and at 0353 increased speed to 28 knots. The two forces now raced along on slightly converging courses. At 0430 visibility had increased to about 12 miles and ten minutes later the *Prince of Wales* was ordered to prepare her Walrus amphibious aircraft for flying. Water in the fuel caused delay so that it was not ready in time and after being damaged by splinters during the action it was jettisoned. At 0510 instant readiness for action was assumed in both ships and at 0537 the *Prince of Wales* reported, 'Enemy in sight distant 17 miles' just as Admiral Holland executed the signal directing both ships to turn 40 degrees to starboard together (280°) to close the range. Four minutes later he stationed the *Prince of Wales* on a bearing of 080°, ie approximately at right angles to the bearing of the enemy. At 0530 the *Bismarck* and *Prinz Eugen* had sighted the smoke of two ships below the horizon to the south-south-east and both prepared for action.

CHAPTER THREE

Action and Reaction

At 0549/24 Admiral Holland ordered his two ships to turn together
20° to starboard which brought them on to a course of 300°, and to
concentrate their fire on the lefthand enemy ship, erroneously believ-
ing that it was the *Bismarck*, the similarity of the silhouettes of the
two ships deceiving him. Fortunately, the Gunnery Control officer
in the *Prince of Wales*, on his own initiative, realised that a mistake
had been made and trained his guns on to the *Bismarck* only seconds
before opening fire. Admiral Holland quickly realised his error and
signalled, 'Shift target right' but it does not appear that this order
reached the Gunnery Control officer in the *Hood*. At 0552½ the
Hood opened fire at an estimated range of 25000 yards, to be followed
half a minute later by the *Prince of Wales*. The turn of 20° towards
the enemy made by the British ships just prior to opening fire closed
their 'A' arcs, that is to say that the after turrets in both ships could
not be trained sufficiently far forward to bear on the target. This
meant that only four of the *Hood*'s eight 15in and six of the *Prince of
Wales*' ten 14in guns were in action at a crucial time. To make
matters worse, one of the last named was only capable of firing one
round because of a defect in the loading mechanism. The enemy,
from whom the British ships were bearing just before his beam,
being under no such handicap, was able to bring the full weight of
his armament to bear against them when at 0555 the two ships
opened fire which was concentrated on the *Hood*. The range was
closing rapidly, and at the same instant as the enemy opened fire
Admiral Holland ordered his two ships to turn together 20° to port
and so enable 'A' arcs to be reopened. When the signal was executed
the *Prince of Wales* had just fired her ninth salvo, having straddled the
Bismarck with her sixth. The first salvo from the last-named ship fell
ahead of the *Hood* and the second astern, but the third was a straddle.
Meanwhile the *Prinz Eugen*, with the more rapid rate of fire of her
8in guns, soon found the range and one of her shells is believed to

have been responsible for starting a fire in the *Hood* amongst the ready-use UP ammunition, ten tons of which was housed in thin steel lockers. The greater part of this was on the boat deck, having been embarked during the ship's brief refit at Devonport in April 1940. As an A/A device the UP rocket was not a success and was later withdrawn from the fleet, but the presence of such a large amount of insufficiently protected explosive in such an exposed position was asking for trouble. The fire spread rapidly forward, but whether or not it contributed to the impending disaster will never be known, but it seems unlikely.

At 0600 Admiral Holland had a signal flying directing his ships to turn a further 20° to port together, the *Hood* had just fired a full salvo and the *Bismarck* her fifth, when horrified watchers in the *Prince of Wales* saw a pillar of flame leap into the air from the after part of the *Hood*, followed by a tremendous explosion which rent the ship in

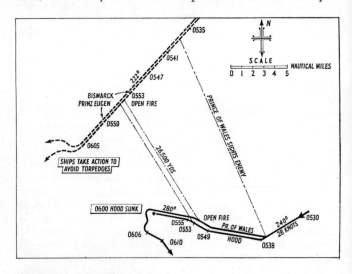

Diagram 2. Plan of action between HMS *Hood* and *Prince of Wales* and the German ships *Bismarck* and *Prinz Eugen* on May 24.

30

two, while a mass of debris soared skywards; then her bow and stern reared up and slid slowly back into the sea, shrouded in a pall of smoke. In a matter of minutes, all that remained of the famous battle-cruiser known throughout the Royal Navy as 'the mighty Hood' was a mass of wreckage. Out of a ship's company of 1418 there were only three survivors, whose rescue an hour and a half later is described below. Another mute witness to the disaster was the Sunderland flying boat from Iceland, which had finally succeeded in making contact with the *Suffolk* just before the action began. After seeing the *Hood* blow up the pilot closed the *Bismarck* in order to identify her and came under heavy A/A fire, but he was able to observe that she was now leaving a broad track of oil, proof of damage received. He emerged from cloud cover just in time to see the *Hood*'s bows disappear and flying over the spot a moment or two later he saw an empty raft painted red surrounded by wreckage in the middle of a large patch of oil. What exactly set off the explosion which caused the *Hood* to disintegrate can only be surmised, but it would seem that a shell must have penetrated one of her magazines. In a letter to *The Times* dated May 26, 1941, the late Admiral of the Fleet Lord Chatfield who, as First Sea Lord and Chief of the Naval Staff from 1933 to 1938 had fought tenaciously but unsuccessfully to persuade the Government of the day to approve a modernisation programme for the obsolescent capital ships in the British fleet, and who was therefore in a strong position to comment on the disaster, made these five points:

1. The *Hood* was not the most powerful warship afloat. True she was the largest, but she was constructed 22 years before the *Bismarck*. In those 22 years engineering science and the power-weight ratio have changed beyond imagination.
2. It cannot be truly said that, 'she was destroyed by a lucky hit'. There are numerous magazines in a capital ship in addition to the four large ones which lie beneath the main turrets. If therefore, a heavy shell penetrates the armour at the angle of descent given by long ranges, the chance of one of the magazines being ignited is quite considerable.
3. The *Hood* was the most powerful ship of her speed that could be constructed in those days. But after the war the sailor made up his mind, after much experiment, that a very fast ship cannot afford to sacrifice armour to get that speed.

4. So in the Nelson class speed was sacrificed to ensure protection against sudden annihilation by shell, torpedo or bomb.

5. Since the *Nelson* was built modern engineering has closed the gap between the two factors.

and he concluded,

'The *Hood* was destroyed because she had to fight a ship 22 years more modern than herself.'

Captain Leach in the *Prince of Wales* had to swing his ship rapidly to starboard to avoid the wreck of the *Hood*. Up till then he had been firing at the *Bismarck* virtually undisturbed, but the latter quickly and accurately shifted the fire of both her main and secondary armament to the new target which she believed was the *King George V* and which was soon surrounded by towering shell splashes, making it difficult for the British battleship's control officer to spot his own fall of shot. It was only a matter of a minute before a 15in shell struck the bridge structure, wrecking it and killing or wounding everyone on it except Captain Leach and his Chief Yeoman of Signals, both of whom, however, were momentarily dazed. The shell did not burst until it emerged on the far side of the bridge structure which was fortunate. During the next few minutes the *Prince of Wales* received a further six hits, three from 15in and three from 8in shell. One of the first named struck the starboard foremost 5.25in director, putting it out of action, another hit the aircraft crane and shattered both wings of the aircraft, the body of which was immediately ditched, while the third pierced the ship's side below the waterline and, after passing through several bulkheads, came to rest without exploding alongside a diesel dynamo room. Two 8in shells hot on the waterline aft, causing a great deal of flooding, while a third entered a 5.25in shell handing room but fortunately again failed to explode. The persistent teething troubles from which the battleship's main armament had suffered throughout the action now began seriously to affect her fire power and, instead of being able to fire five gun salvoes they were mostly only of three. The contractors' men who were still onboard did their utmost in the totally unforeseen circumstances with which they were confronted, to keep the guns in action, but they only achieved partial success. The range was now down to 14500 yards and with the enemy's rate and accuracy of fire still apparently un-impaired, at 0613 Captain Leach decided to break off the action and

Top: The *Bismarck* in a Norwegian Fiord, taken from the *Prinz Eugen. Above:* Sister ship to *Prinz Eugen.* Hipper Class

Above: The mystery of the whereabouts of the German battleship *Bismarck* was solved by this reconnaissance photograph taken by an aircraft of Coastal Command. It revealed her in Dobric Fjord just before she weighed anchor for her first and last sortie. She was finally destroyed by the Royal Navy

Left: The *Prinz Eugen* spotted in Hjelte Fjord

Opposite: Admiral Lutjens inspecting the crew of the *Prinz Eugen*

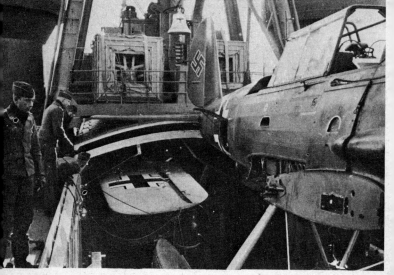

From Left to Right: Grossadmiral Erich Raeder, Head of the German Navy. Admiral Lutjens, in command of operation 'Rhineübung'. Scene aboard the *Prinz Eugen*. Taking bearings

Left: Spotting seaplane Arado A96 being prepared for launching from the *Prinz Eugen*

Above: HMS *Suffolk* the cruiser which first sighted the *Bismarck*

Top: British Battle Cruiser *Hood. Above:* The *Bismarck* in action against HMS *Hood.* Taken from the *Prinz Eugen* on May 24, 1941

Opposite, top: The *Bismarck* engaging the *Hood.* Taken from the *Prinz Eugen* on May 24, 1941. *Opposite, centre:* The *Bismarck* engaging HMS *Hood.* Taken from the *Prinz Eugen. Opposite, foot:* Shell from HMS *Hood* bursting near the *Bismarck*, photograph taken from the *Prinz Eugen* on May 24, 1941

Top: HMS *Hood* is hit. HMS *Prince of Wales* in company. Taken from the *Prinz Eugen*. *Above:* HMS *Hood* blows up. In background HMS *Prince of Wales*. Taken from *Prinz Eugen*

Opposite, top: Admiral Sir John Tovey with Captain J. C. Leach, RN on board HMS *Prince of Wales*. *Opposite, foot:* HMS *Repulse*

Top: HMS *Renown*, flagship of Admiral Sir James Somerville KCB. *Above:* HMS *Norfolk*, flagship of Rear Admiral Wake-Walker

Opposite, Top: Vice Admiral Sir W. Frederic Wake-Walker KCB, CBE. *Opposite, Foot:* The aircraft carrier HMS *Ark Royal*

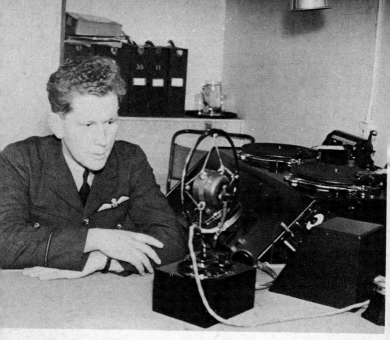

Opposite, top: Aerial view of British 23000-ton aircraft carrier HMS *Victorious* with Albacores ranged on the flight deck. *Opposite, foot:* Flying Officer D. A. Briggs, the captain of the Catalina flying boat which resighted the *Bismarck* and broke cloud cover 400 yards from her while attempting to shadow the German battleship. The *Bismarck* put up a terrific anti-aircraft barrage which forced him to take violent avoiding action. The hull of his flying boat was holed in several places, but the crew plugged the holes and the flying boat continued to shadow the German battleship for ten hours longer.

Left: Captain P. Vian on the bridge of HMS *Cossack*. *Below:* Aerial view of HMS *King George V*

Left: Admiral Sir J. Tovey KCB, KBE, DSO Commander in Chief Home Fleet on the quarter deck of his flagship

Top: HMS *King George V*, flagship of Admiral Sir John Tovey. *Centre:* HMS *Rodney* with 16in gun turrets trained ready for action. *Above:* 16in shells from HMS *Rodney* falling astern of *Bismarck*

Top: The *Bismarck* underway after
being crippled. *Centre: Bismarck*—an
oily streak and an ominous sky.
Photographed by shadowing aircraft.
Above: Bismarck action. *Bismarck* on fire
at the closing stages of the battle

retire under cover of smoke. He altered course to 160° and during the turn the shell ring of the after 14in turret which was still firing at the *Bismarck* jammed, and it was not until 0720 that two of the guns were back in action and another hour before the other two could be loaded. Captain Leach gave three main reasons for breaking off the engagement:

(a) the mechanical troubles which prevented the main armament from producing a full output.

(b) his ship had only just reached the stage of being reasonably fit to take part in service operations.

(c) the likelihood of a decisive concentration being effected later.

He went on to say that he did not consider it sound tactics to continue single-handed the engagement with the two German ships, both of which might be expected to be at the peak of their efficiency. As a result of the damage she had received the *Prince of Wales* had shipped 400 tons of water, and her speed was reduced to 27 knots. Rear-Admiral Wake-Walker, who had now succeeded to the command of the force, fully approved Captain Leach's action. At 0630 he signalled his intention of maintaining touch and he ordered the *Prince of Wales* to open out to a distance of ten miles on a bearing of 110° so that he could fall back on her if attacked. At 0637 he ordered the destroyers *Electra*, *Echo*, *Icarus* and *Achates* to search for survivors of the *Hood*. They were 30 miles north of the scene of the action as a result of Admiral Holland's decision to detach them when he turned south and it was 0745 before they reached the position where the *Hood* had blown up. A dramatic account of the rescue of the only three survivors is given in the book HMS *Electra*, a ship with a war record unique in the annals of naval warfare. After describing how she raced south expecting to find hundreds of survivors in boats, on rafts or swimming about in the water, those on her bridge sighted, 'quite suddenly, on the rolling swell, a large patch of oil ahead, a tangled pile of small wreckage . . . *and that was all* . . . far over to starboard we saw three men—two of them swimming, one on a raft. But in the chilling waters around them there was no other sign of life'.* After recovering the three men, one of whom was a Midshipman, the *Electra* and the other destroyers searched the area until 0900 when they set course for Hvalfiord where they arrived at 2000 that night.

* HMS *Electra* by Lieutenant Commander T. J. Cain RN (Rtd.) as told to A. V. Sellwood. F. Muller Ltd., 1959.

The *Bismarck* did not attempt to continue the action. She had received two severe hits and one minor one from the *Prince of Wales'* guns one of which pierced compartment 13/14 and put No 4 dynamo out of action, as well as causing a slight leak in number 2 boiler room, the other entering compartment 20/21, pierced a fuel tank causing a serious leak of oil as well as contaminating fuel in adjacent tanks. Five men were wounded and the ship's speed reduced to 28 knots. The *Prinz Eugen*, believed to have been the target of the *Hood*'s guns during her brief period in action, escaped undamaged. Admiral Lütjens was now faced with a difficult decision. He could either continue the action with the risk of further damage or attempt to break back through the Denmark Straits in the hope of reaching a German port. Alternatively he could continue into the Atlantic in the hope of throwing off his shadowers and then make for a port on the west coast of France, bearing in mind that only at St Nazaire was there a dry dock large enough to take the *Bismarck*. He evidently decided on the second course and at 0901 made a signal to this effect to Group West at the same time reporting the damage suffered by his flagship. Admiral Raeder says that he fully agreed with the decision and he stoutly defended Lütjens' action when, on June 6, he reported to Hitler the tragic outcome of the operation. Hitler on the other hand, criticised him for not continuing the action and finishing off the *Prince of Wales*. A German historian has written:

'If he had had the slightest suspicion that his target was the *Prince of Wales* which was still in the testing stage, manned by a totally inexperienced crew with some shipyard personnel still onboard, and working to overcome "bugs", he would hardly have permitted her to escape.'*

Be that as it may, and even if, as another writer suggests† Captain Lindeman did not agree with his admiral's decision though he too thought he had been engaged with the *King George V*, it must remain a matter for speculation, since no one with a knowledge of what was in the Admiral's mind survived.

When the news of the loss of the *Hood* reached the Admiralty a

* *Exploits and end of the Bismarck* by Commander (later Captain) Grenard Bidlingmaier, Federal Germany Navy. US Naval Institute Proceedings, July 1958, pp. 77–87.
† *The German Navy in World War II* by Edward P. von der Porten, p. 156. Arthur Barker Ltd, London.

number of dispositions were made to meet possible eventualities. At 0120/24 the cruisers *Manchester, Birmingham* and *Arethusa* were ordered to proceed with despatch to patrol off Langanaes (north-east point of Iceland); the battleship *Rodney* which, with four destroyers was escorting the west-bound liner *Britannic*, was ordered at 1022/24 to close the enemy on a westerly course, leaving one destroyer with the *Britannic*. Detailing the *Eskimo* for this duty, she took the *Somali, Tartar* and *Mashona* with her. She was on her way to Boston USA for a much needed refit and had onboard a number of officer and rating passengers who included some cases of shell-shock and invalids bound for hospitals in Canada. Her upper deck was encumbered with several cases of spare parts needed during the refit and two extra large ones, each containing an eight barrelled pom-pom mounting. She had not been refitted for over two years and her main engines and boilers were full of leaks as a result of prolonged high speed steaming during the first months of the war. But despite all these handicaps she was to play a very important part in the events about to take place.

The battleship *Ramillies* escorting an eastbound convoy, at 1144/24 was ordered to place herself westward of the enemy ship who was estimated to be 900 miles to the north of her, and the battleship *Revenge* at Halifax was instructed at 1917/24 to sail and close the position of the enemy. The cruiser *Edinburgh* on patrol in mid-Atlantic was ordered at 1250/24 to close the enemy and take over as a relief shadower.

Throughout the forenoon of the 24th the *Bismarck* proceeded in a south-westerly direction trying hard by frequent alterations of course to throw off the persistent British cruisers. The visibility was variable, between two and seventeen miles, but the *Suffolk*, with the help of her radar maintained station on her starboard quarter and so fore-stalling any attempt on the part of the enemy to break back along the ice edge unobserved, while the *Norfolk* and the *Prince of Wales* kept on the port quarter. At 1320 the *Bismarck* altered course to south and reduced speed to 24 knots. This was welcome news to Admiral Tovey who, up till then had been anxious lest the enemy ships should turn westwards and rendezvous with a tanker off Greenland where, unknown to him there were in fact two waiting, 120 and 200 miles south of Cape Farewell. The Commander-in-Chief was not aware of the extent of the damage received by the *Bismarck* during the action other than that she was leaving an appreciable trail of oil.

There was of course, the possibility that Admiral Lütjens was leading the British ships towards a concentration of U-boats but it seemed unlikely that he was aware of the presence of other heavy ships at sea in the area. The chances of interception by the *King George V* had now much improved, but it was important to reduce the *Bismarck's* speed to make sure of bringing her to action. At 1440 Admiral Tovey detached Rear-Admiral A.T.B. Curteis commanding the 2nd Cruiser Squadron, with his flag in the 6in gun cruiser *Galatea* with the carrier *Victorious* and the cruisers *Aurora*, *Kenya* and *Hermione*, with orders to get within 100 miles of the *Bismarck* as soon as possible and launch a Torpedo/Bomber attack on her. It appeared to him that if the *Bismarck* continued on her present course and at the same speed he would be able to make contact with her about 0900/25, half an hour after sunrise when the light would be favourable to an approach from the eastward.

At 1535 a Catalina aircraft which was in sight from the *Norfolk* sighted the *Bismarck* without apparently herself being seen, and reported the enemy battleship as 15 miles ahead preceded by the *Prinz Eugen*. About this time Admiral Lütjens made his first attempt to detach the *Prinz Eugen* but something went wrong and the two ships found themselves in company again. At 1711 Admiral Wake-Walker ordered the *Prince of Wales* to take station ahead of the *Norfolk* with a view to trying to slow down the enemy by attacking her from astern, and at 1809 he ordered the *Suffolk* to close in to five miles. His plan was, however, frustrated by the enemy. At about 1830 a rain squall enveloped the enemy ships and Admiral Lütjens decided this was the moment to make a second attempt to detach the *Prinz Eugen*. At 1839 he ordered the *Bismarck* to reverse her course and round on her shadowers. At the time the *Suffolk* was about 13 miles to the north of her and fortunately was on the lookout for such a move. She put her helm hard over and swung round on to an opposite course on which she steadied just as the *Bismarck*, emerging from the mist, opened fire on her. The shots fell short, although two near misses started rivets in the side plating aft. She made smoke and opened fire, being supported at long range by the *Norfolk* and *Prince of Wales*, two of whose guns again went out of action. Her object achieved, the *Bismarck* broke off the action and turned west, later resuming a southerly course.

The German Naval High Command had suspended all U-boat operations against shipping for the duration of Operation Rheinübung in case the submarines were needed to co-operate with the surface ships, and an experienced U-boat officer had been appointed to Admiral Lütjens' staff. Presumably on his advice, at 1442 the Admiral had ordered U-boats to concentrate 340 miles south of Cape Farewell (Greenland) at dawn on the 25th, hoping to lead his persistent shadowers over them. Group West had also suggested that he should make for some remote area and lie low for a while, but the Admiral seems to have discarded both these projects when he realised how serious was the loss of fuel as a result of the damage sustained during the action. In any case it seemed impossible to escape from his pursuers and at 2056 he signalled that he was proceeding direct to Brest owing to the fuel situation.

Meanwhile, at 1509 Rear-Admiral Curteis had taken the ships assigned to him under his orders and, parting company with the Commander-in-Chief, was proceeding at 28 knots to carry out his instructions, hoping to be in a position to launch an attack on the enemy battleship at 2100. However, although the navigating officer of the *Galatea* had obtained an astronomical fix at 2000 it had not been possible to co-ordinate the geographical position of his force with that of the shadowing cruisers, further the westerly side-step made by the *Bismarck* after her brush with the *Prince of Wales* and the two cruisers soon made it evident that the force would not reach a position within 100 miles of the enemy before about 2300. Nevertheless Admiral Curteis decided to launch the striking force at 2200 when he estimated he would be about 120 miles away from the target. At 2208 the *Victorious* altered course to 300° and reduced speed to 15 knots to fly off her nine Swordfish aircraft of 825 squadron, each armed with an 18in torpedo fitted with a Duplex pistol and set to run at a depth of 31 feet. The weather was squally with occasional showers, the wind being fresh from the northwest, and visibility good. But as seen from the flying deck the prospect was not encouraging, the sea looked dark and forbidding under a leaden sky and scudding clouds. The squadron led by Lieutenant-Commander Eugene Esmonde RN (later to earn a posthumous VC for his gallant attack against the *Scharnhorst*) set course 225° at 85 knots and sighted the *Bismarck* through a gap in the clouds at 2330, having picked her up by radar three minutes previously, then the cloud thickened and she was lost to view. A United States coastguard cutter in the vicinity caused some confusion but with the help of the *Norfolk* the battleship was relocated and at 2350 the formation broke cloud to deliver its attack. The *Bismarck* sighted the aircraft at a range of six miles and opened a heavy barrage fire but the attacks were pressed home with great gallantry from all directions by eight of the nine aircraft and it was believed that a hit was scored on the battleship's starboard side abreast the bridge. The German report admitting this stated that it had no effect on the ship's combat readiness which was true, but it appears that the violent turns made by the ship to avoid the torpedoes, coupled with the heavy gunfire, opened up the leak in number 2 boiler room which had to be abandoned and speed was temporarily reduced to 16 knots. A Fulmar reconnaissance aircraft flown off at 2300 observed a column of black smoke rising from the ship which was no doubt due to the sudden reduction in speed, and reported that she seemed to have slowed down. Great difficulty was experienced in recovering the strike aircraft due to a breakdown of *Victorious'* homing beacon, and searchlights had to be burned, but by 0215/25 all aircraft except two Fulmars had been recovered and the crews of these last two were subsequently picked up.

Contact Lost With the Bismarck

To Admiral Tovey the news of a probable hit on the *Bismarck* was most welcome, but it would not be known for some time whether or not it had reduced her speed. While awaiting confirmation of this a most untoward event occurred. The *Suffolk*, having the better radar set, had been ordered at 0145 to act independently, while the *Norfolk* with the *Prince of Wales* astern followed to give close support. The *Bismarck* was now steering a course of 160° at a speed of 16 knots. At 0229 she bore 192° distant 10½ miles from the *Suffolk* which was zig-zagging 30 degrees on either side of the mean line of advance and losing touch on the outward legs but regaining it on the inward ones. The effect on a tired crew was to engender a feeling of over confidence. After contact at 0306 the *Suffolk* turned away, at which instant the *Bismarck* altered course sharply to starboard so that when the cruiser, after the customary ten minutes on the outward leg turned inwards there was no sign of the enemy. By 0401 when Captain Ellis was obliged to recognise the unpleasant fact that the battleship had given him the slip, he reported the fact adding that he was acting on the

Diagram 3. (*Opposite*) *Bismarck* lost after torpedo attacks by *Victorious'* aircraft.

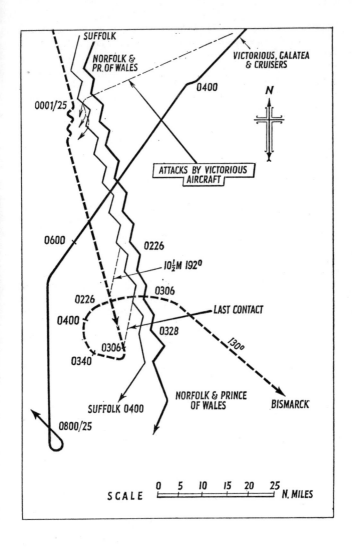

SUFFOLK

NORFOLK &
PR. OF WALES

VICTORIOUS, GALATEA
& CRUISERS

N

0400

0001/25

ATTACKS BY VICTORIOUS
AIRCRAFT

0600

0226

$10\frac{1}{2}$M 192°

0226

0306

LAST CONTACT

0400

0306

0328

130°

0340

SUFFOLK 0400

NORFOLK & PRINCE
OF WALES

BISMARCK

0800/25

SCALE 0 5 10 15 20 25 N. MILES

assumption that she had turned west. The *Norfolk* herself had not had contact with the *Bismarck* for two hours and at 0552 Admiral Wake-Walker asked Admiral Tovey if the *Victorious* could carry out an air search in this direction at dawn. The *Bismarck* had in fact turned almost a complete circle from south through west to north and east, finally steadying on a course of approximately 130°.

CHAPTER FOUR

Pursuit

All hopes of bringing the *Bismarck* to action on the forenoon of May 25 faded with the receipt of the news that contact had been lost, which reached Admiral Tovey at 0605 that morning. It appeared to him that she might be doing one of three things:

(a) making a rendezvous with a tanker, possibly off the east coast of Greenland, or somewhere further south, like the Azores or Canary Islands.

(b) making for a dockyard on the west coast of France or possibly an Italian port in the Mediterranean.

(c) returning to Germany for repairs.

In default of further information it had to be assumed that her speed was unimpaired and as she had complete freedom of movement a wide area of search would have to be covered if all possible courses of action were to be met. For this, the forces at his disposal were quite inadequate, especially long-range aircraft which were in very short supply at that time. He therefore had to decide which of the above courses was the most dangerous from the British point of view and it was clearly course (a) since with her fuel tanks replenished the *Bismarck* would be able to start operations against shipping which it must be supposed was the object of her sortie. He therefore decided to concentrate his efforts on searching an area between south through west to north-west from the *Bismarck*'s last reported position. As already noted, Rear-Admiral Wake-Walker's two cruisers had anticipated this action, the *Suffolk* having started to search in a south-westerly direction (230°) at 25 knots, while the *Norfolk* searched to the westward at daylight. At 0630 the *Prince of Wales* was detached to join the Commander-in-Chief.

At 0630 Admiral Tovey ordered Rear-Admiral Curteis, who was now steering with his force towards the *Bismarck*'s last reported position, to direct the *Victorious* to carry out a dawn search to the north-west and to spread his cruisers and sweep in that direction. The message was received at 0716 just as the carrier was preparing to carry out an air search to the eastward, timed to begin at 0730. During the night five Fulmars had been launched to maintain touch with the enemy, but without success. Two of these, as already mentioned, had failed to return, so only seven Swordfish were now available to carry out the search and these were launched at 0810 with orders to cover a sector between 280° and 040° to a depth of 100 miles to comply with the Commander-in-Chief's instructions. The battle-cruiser *Repulse* reported that she was getting short of fuel, so at 0906 Admiral Tovey detached her with orders to proceed to Newfoundland to replenish, covering on passage part of the westerly search sector. Then at 1047 information was received which called for a complete change of plan, but before considering it it is necessary to review the movements of the other ships at sea in the Atlantic.

The battleship *Rodney*, Captain F. H. G. Dalrymple-Hamilton RN, which had been steering to the southwest to intercept the *Bismarck*, and which was at this time 350 miles southeast of her last reported position, received the signal reporting that contact had been lost. Finding that she was in an excellent position to cut off the enemy ship were she heading for a French port or even one in northern Spain, her captain decided to cruise in his present area until further news was received.

The battleship *Ramillies*, Captain A. D. Read RN, the top speed of which was not more than 19 knots, was some 400 miles south of the position where the *Bismarck* had given her shadowers the slip, and was steering to the northwest in accordance with the instructions previously received from the Admiralty. The cruiser *Edinburgh*, Captain C. M. Blackman RN, 300 miles southeast of the *Ramillies*, was steering towards the enemy's last reported position and in so doing was covering part of the southeast sector of the enemy's possible line of advance. Further south the cruiser *London*, Captain R. M. Servaes RN, was searching for a possible enemy supply ship in the Canary Islands area.

Vice-Admiral Somerville with Force H was pressing on to the northward and at 1300/25 was 320 miles due west of Cape Finisterre

Diagram 4. (*Opposite*) Movements of British Forces after losing touch with *Bismarck* 0800–2000 on May 25.

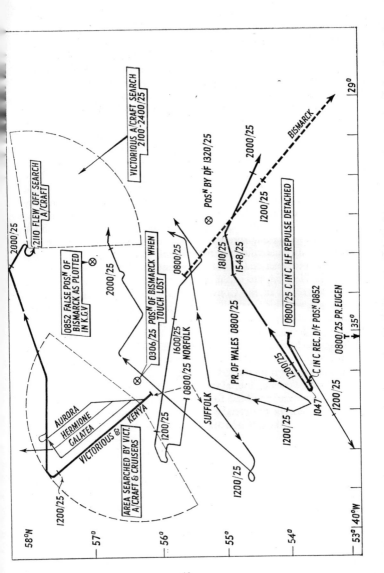

VICTORIOUS A/CRAFT SEARCH 2100-2400/25

2110 FLEW OFF SEARCH A/CRAFT

2000/25

0852 FALSE POSⁿ OF BISMARCK AS PLOTTED IN K.G.V.

2000/25

POSⁿ BY D/F 1320/25

2000/25

1200/25

BISMARCK

1810/25

1548/25

0306/25 POSⁿ OF BISMARCK WHEN TOUCH LOST

0800/25

0800/25 C IN C H.F REPULSE DETACHED

PR. OF WALES 0800/25

1600/25 NORFOLK

1200/25

0800/25 C IN C REC. D/F POSⁿ 0852

0800/25 PR.EUGEN

1047

1200/25

2000/25

1200/25

AURORA
HERMIONE
GALATEA

VICTORIOUS & VICT. KENYA

1200/25

0800/25

SUFFOLK

1200/25

AREA SEARCHED BY VICT. A/CRAFT & CRUISERS

1200/25

1200/25

58°N

57°

56°

55°

54°

53° 40°W

29°

35°

43

and so in a good position to intercept the *Bismarck* should she be heading for Brest or Ferrol, which he thought was a likely alternative.

Onboard the *Bismarck* at 0800/25 Admiral Lütjens, still unaware that the shadowing cruisers had lost touch apparently because radar pulses were still being picked up, though this did not necessarily mean that the sender was receiving any echo, despatched an amplifying account of the action with the *Hood* which took some thirty minutes to transmit. Watchful British Direction Finding stations took bearings of this transmission which, when plotted, showed that the *Bismarck* was well east of her last reported position. Unfortunately, instead of giving Admiral Tovey the position thus obtained, the actual bearings were passed to him and these were plotted on a Mercators chart, although bearings obtained by radio follow a great circle path along the surface of the earth. The false position thus obtained put the *Bismarck* 200 miles north of her true position and from this the Commander-in-Chief deduced that she was trying to return to Germany through the Iceland–Faroes channel. So at 1047, shortly after detaching the *Repulse*, he altered the course of his force to the northeast and set off in pursuit, at the same time telling all Home Fleet ships to adjust their searches accordingly.

On receipt of the Commander-in-Chief's signal, Rear-Admiral Curteis with his four cruisers turned to the eastward (085°), leaving the *Victorious*, the search of whose aircraft to the northwest had proved fruitless, to recover them. At 1107 she landed on six Swordfish, one having failed to return, and after calling the missing aircraft for some time, she also turned east and prepared to launch a further search. Other ships reacted similarly. The *Prince of Wales*, steering to close the fleet flagship, altered course for the Denmark Straits; the *Ramillies* changed course from north to east-north-east, although she could not hope to overtake the much faster enemy ship; the *Rodney* which at 1108 had been ordered by the Admiralty to act on the assumption that the *Bismarck* was making for Brest, was in something of a quandary, but at 1200, having regained her three destroyers which had dropped back owing to bad weather, set off on a course of 055°. Two and a half hours later, at 1428, the Admiralty ordered the *Rodney* to comply with the Commander-in-Chief's message timed 1047, which she was now doing, then at 1805 the message timed 1428 was cancelled and she was told to act on the assumption that the enemy ship was making for a French port. This series of signals shows the difficulty experienced in reaching a conclusion regarding the *Bismarck*'s most probable course of action. Rear-Admiral Wake-Walker was convinced in his own mind that the *Bismarck* would be making for Brest so he compromised by steering a course a little to the south of east (100°), while the *Suffolk* steered towards Iceland. The cruiser *Edinburgh* apparently too far south to be of much use in what now appeared to be a stern chase, began a curve of search in case the enemy should be making for Brest.

Admiral Somerville, whose Force H was not strictly a part of the Home Fleet and who had intercepted Admiral Tovey's message timed 1047, now received one from the Admiralty timed 1100 ordering him to assume that the *Bismarck* was making for Brest, altered course to 337° and instructed the *Ark Royal* to prepare to carry out an extensive air search. Meanwhile that afternoon three Catalina aircraft of Coastal Command began a search of the area through which it was considered probable the *Bismarck* might be steaming. They continued their searches for an average of just over 20 hours but failed to sight the enemy though one of them during the night sighted a warship which could not be identified and low cloud prevented the use of a parachute flare.

At 1320 the Admiralty obtained bearings of an enemy transmission which was in fact made by a U-boat reporting having sighted the *Victorious* and which appeared to fit in with the assumption that the *Bismarck* was making for the French coast. It might have been suspected from the radio frequency employed that it was unlikely that it emanated from the *Bismarck*, but it was passed to Admiral Tovey for what it was worth, and reached him at 1530. But an hour earlier he had intercepted the Admiralty's signal timed 1428 to the *Rodney* telling her to comply with his instructions to search to the north-eastward, so he was in some doubt as to what the Admiralty's appreciation of the enemy's intended movement really was. Meanwhile, the error in the plotting of the 0852 D/F position had been discovered and this, taken in conjunction with the one just received, seemed to indicate that the *Bismarck* was not seeking to return to Germany by the Iceland–Faroes passage. After a thorough re-appreciation in the light of the little information available, he decided at 1810 to alter course to the east-south-eastward (118°). Just over an hour later, at 1924, the Admiralty informed all ships that it was now the considered opinion of the naval staff that the *Bismarck* was making for a French west coast port. As a result of the false scent which he had been following for just over seven hours, the quarry was now

150 miles to the east of the Home Fleet flagship, but she still had nearly 1000 miles to go to reach her destination.

Admiral Lütjens had reason to believe that at last he had evaded his pursuers but he fully realised that he would be very lucky to reach his destination without opposition. It was the German Admiral's birthday and at 1152 Admiral Raeder sent him greetings with the hope that he would, 'continue to be equally successful in the coming year'. Somewhat later Hitler sent him his best wishes, and the Admiral took the opportunity when thanking his flagship's company over the loud hailer system for their greetings to remind them the worst was yet to come since it was hardly likely that the British would not strain every nerve to avenge the loss of the *Hood* and that the *Bismarck* might still be called upon to fight a life or death struggle. It appears from survivors' reports that this speech engendered deep pessimism amongst the younger members of the ship's company who were in the majority, and it did nothing to strengthen morale.

After close consultation between the Commander-in-Chief Coastal Command, Air Chief Marshal Sir Frederick Bowhill—himself an old sailor—and the Admiralty naval staff, it was decided to establish during daylight on the 26th, two cross-over patrols covering the approaches to the Bay of Biscay, using Catalina aircraft equipped with long-range tanks. The northern one would take care of possible enemy courses between Brest and the middle of the Bay, while the southern one covered from the middle of the Bay to Cape Finisterre. A patrol by six submarines was also established 120 miles to the west of Brest and later that evening it was moved south to take in the approaches to St Nazaire.

During the night of 25/26th the weather deteriorated considerably. The wind from the northwest rose to gale force, whipping up a nasty sea which added to the difficulty of high-speed steaming. The visibility was reduced from time to time by heavy rain squalls and dark clouds scudded low over the surface of the turbulent sea. Although during the forenoon of the 25th the Admiralty had placed the *Rodney* and the *Ramillies* under his orders, Admiral Tovey had no accurate information of their whereabouts. The first named had not reported her position since that forenoon and during the same afternoon the latter had been withdrawn to escort the liner *Britannic* which had originally had the *Rodney* for escort. In fact, the Admiralty was now so uncertain of the position of the many isolated ships in the area of operations that since 0600/25 the sending out of situation reports had been discontinued for fear that they might be so inaccurate as to be misleading, although up to that time they had proved of great value.

So as on the gloomy and stormy morning of May 25 Admiral Tovey surveyed the situation, it was not an encouraging picture which presented itself. Shortage of fuel had begun to cause him serious concern and at 2238 the previous evening he had felt it necessary to warn the Admiralty that he might have to reduce speed to economise fuel. He was now without a destroyer screen as the seven ships carrying out this duty had left him to replenish in Iceland, as also had the *Prince of Wales*; the *Victorious* and the four cruisers with her, on completion of the day's search had had to follow suit, and moreover there were no destroyers to screen the carrier. It seemed to him that everything now depended on Force H hurrying northward. The *Ark Royal*, with her experienced and fully trained air crews might prove invaluable in reducing the enemy's speed and so enable the *King George V* to overtake her and bring her to action. But the nearer the *Bismarck* got to the French coast the easier it would be for German aircraft and submarines to come to her aid, and since he was without a destroyer screen this could be a serious menace.

Unknown to him, the previous day Group West had informed Admiral Lütjens that Focke Wulf 200 aircraft would carry out reconnaissance as far as possible to the west and that strong air forces were available to cover the *Bismarck* when she reached longitude 14° west. Seven U-boats, later amended to five, were established on patrol 300 miles to the west of Brest. At 2230/25 Admiral Tovey had asked the Admiralty what chances there were of making some destroyers available both for the *King George V* and the *Rodney*, for although he knew that the latter had had three destroyers in company, he assumed that by now they also would have had to leave to refuel. The Admiralty fully appreciated Admiral Tovey's anxiety, and decided to denude troop convoy WS.8B of its escort of five destroyers and send them to join the Commander-in-Chief. It was a calculated risk but in the circumstances, fully justified, as according to the latest intelligence there were no U-boats in the vicinity of the convoy which at that time (midnight May 25/26) was only 240 miles to the southeast of the *King George V*. The five destroyers were part of the 4th Destroyer flotilla commanded by the redoubtable Captain (later Admiral of the Fleet Sir Philip) Vian in the *Cossack* and it was decided to send him with *Sikh* and *Zulu* to join the *King George V*, and the *Maori* with the Polish manned destroyer *Piorun*, to join the *Rodney*. As the convoy was under the operational control of the Commander-in-Chief Western Approaches, the Admiralty told him to issue the necessary instructions, and he managed to find a sixth destroyer, the *Jupiter*, exercising in the Irish Sea, which was also told to join Admiral Tovey but of course, having a much greater distance to go, she could not arrive as soon as the other five. At 0200/26 a signal was despatched giving effect to the above movements.

To Admiral Somerville, whose Force H was now approaching the scene of operations, the re-location of the *Bismarck* was naturally uppermost in his mind, but he had very little information to work on other than that she was making in the general direction of Brest. After consulting by signal with Captain Maund of the *Ark Royal*, it was decided to fly off the first air search at daylight on the 26th, orientated to cover possible enemy speeds between 25 and 21 knots. If that search were unsuccessful, another one beginning about 1300 would be launched to cover speeds down to 18 knots, and if that too failed, a third one covering speeds down to 15 knots would be flown off. There was another matter too which was causing him some concern. He knew that the German battle-cruisers *Scharnhorst* and *Gneisenau* had gone into Brest after their Atlantic foray and that they had been bombed there, but he was not aware if they were fit to put to sea to join forces with the *Bismarck* as it will be recalled, was Admiral Raeder's original intention. He therefore took the opportunity at 0900 on the morning of the 26th, when he was obliged to detach his destroyers to return to Gibraltar to refuel, to order the senior officer to make two signals when 150 miles clear of the *Renown*, one addressed to the Admiralty gave his position, course and speed at 0730/26, the other addressed to the Commander-in-Chief Plymouth requested information about the most recent reconnaissance of Brest. Due to changing radio frequencies, information to the effect that both ships were still in harbour at 1930/25 did not reach him in time to prevent the launching of a security patrol at 7716/26 to search to the north and west.

The north-westerly gale which was causing the *King George V* to corkscrew uncomfortably as she steamed eastward at 24 knots with the sea on her port quarter, impeded the progress of Force H steering almost head on into it. During the night speed had to be reduced progressively from 25 to 23, to 19 knots and finally during the middle watch (0000 to 0400) to 17 knots. Even at this speed the *Renown* was taking in green seas over her forecastle, while the *Ark Royal*'s flying deck, unceasingly swept by spray, was pitching with a rise and fall as measured by sextant at the stern of over 50 feet. In peace time, under such conditions it would have been out of the question to attempt to operate aircraft but in war risks have to be taken. The reduction in speed during the night had delayed the carrier's arrival at the planned point of departure for the first of the searches for the *Bismarck* and as a compromise, Captain Maund obtained Admiral Somerville's permission to move the search area 35 miles to the southeast. This enabled launching to begin at 0830 instead of 0900. Ranging aircraft on the wet, slippery, pitching deck was most hazardous but it was accomplished without accident. At 0835 the ship turned into the eye of the wind and reduced speed to 10 knots so that launching could begin. One by one the ten Swordfish aircraft detailed for the first search opened their throttles and moving in fits and starts along the see-sawing deck, gathered flying speed and took off. Immediately six more Swordfish in the hangar, already fitted with long-range tanks, were prepared for launching should the *Bismarck* be sighted. Meanwhile the ship herself altered course to north and headed for the rendezvous 50 miles away to which the aircraft had been ordered to return.

CHAPTER FIVE

May 26 — Bismarck Relocated

But it was not to *Ark Royal*'s gallant Swordfish crews that the honour of relocating the *Bismarck* was to be accorded. Five hours before they had made their perilous take-off, at 0300/26 two Catalina aircraft of Coastal Command had set out from their base on Lough Erne in Northern Ireland to begin the cross-over patrols in the Bay of Biscay referred to above. Gradually darkness gave way to daylight and the crews were able to see below them the white topped waves of the gale-swept ocean as they flew on hour after hour to reach their initial positions. Suddenly at 1030, when flying at a height of only 500 feet, the pilot of Catalina A of 209 Squadron, Fying Officer D. A. Briggs, on the southernmost of the two patrols, sighted the dark grey hull of a warship. Because she was alone and without destroyer escort he assumed it must be the *Bismarck* (though unknown to him it might equally well have been the *King George V* or *Rodney*) and he sent off a signal to this effect. The Catalina then took cover in a cloud but nine minutes later broke through right above the battleship which promptly opened fire, fortunately without scoring a hit though the aircraft's hull was holed by a number of splinters, one of which passed between the First and Second pilots. In taking avoiding action, the Catalina temporarily lost touch, but fortunately *Ark Royal*'s search aircraft were approaching from the southeast and half an hour later one of the Swordfish sighted the same ship which was reported as an enemy cruiser. In accordance with the standard procedure whereby any aircraft making contact with an enemy vessel is immediately joined by the one next to her, another Swordfish moved over and on sighting the ship reported her as a battleship.

To the senior officers at sea and to the Naval Staff at the Admiralty

Diagram 5. (*Opposite*) *Bismarck* relocated, movements of British Forces from 1030 on May 26.

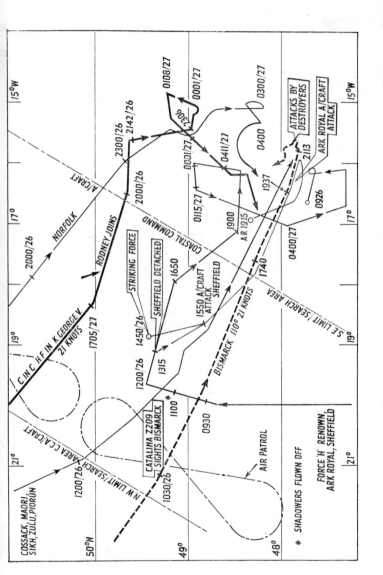

the most welcome news of the sighting was tempered by the doubts raised by the several aircraft regarding her identity. Was it the *Prinz Eugen* or the *Bismarck*? The similar silhouettes of the two ships had caused confusion before when they were in company, now they were separated it was more difficult to tell them apart, especially from the air. Although the pilots of the first two Swordfish, when interrogated after their return to the carrier, could not definitely identify the ship they had sighted, the Swordfish which had relieved them soon confirmed beyond doubt that she was indeed the *Bismarck*. The position of the *Bismarck* as given in Catalina Z's sighting report (and subsequently found to have placed her 25 miles too far to the west) located her 690 miles 277° from Brest, 135 miles due south of the *King George V*, 125 miles south by west from the *Rodney*, and 112 miles west-north-west from the *Renown*. It showed that she was making good about 20 knots and at that speed by daylight on the 27th she would be within range of support from the German Air Force. The *King George V* had insufficient speed to close within range of her during daylight that day and for the even slower *Rodney* it was out of the question. Only Force H was in a position to challenge the *Bismarck* during her final dash for safety, but the *Renown* alone could not take her on. It was essential that she be slowed down to allow the two battleships to catch up and this meant she must be crippled by torpedoes launched by *Ark Royal*'s aircraft or possibly Captain Vian's destroyers.

It was evident to the Admiralty too, that only Force H stood between the *Bismarck* and her goal, and knowing the fighting propensities of Admiral Somerville, at 1052 they sent him a definite order that the *Renown* was not to engage the *Bismarck* unless she was already engaged with the *King George V* or *Rodney*. He therefore concentrated all his efforts on launching an air strike against her at the earliest possible moment. Before this could be done, eight search aircraft—two having remained as shadowers—had to be landed on, refuelled and rearmed. This in the prevailing weather might take some time, but by noon it was safely accomplished, with the destruction of only one aircraft which had the misfortune to be caught in the upsurge of the after end of the flying deck just as it was attempting to land, and was severely damaged.

Force H had now crossed the *Bismarck*'s line of advance and was at noon about 50 miles to the northeast of her estimated position. Since the *Ark Royal* would have to steam into the eye of the wind both when launching and landing on aircraft, it was of the greatest importance to ensure that she did not get too close to or too far away from the *Bismarck* during the operation. With the wind in the north-west the position which Admiral Somerville had taken up fulfilled all these conditions. The ground lost when head to wind could be recovered between flying off and landing on by steaming down wind at high speed and without getting too close to the enemy ship on his south-easterly course. By 1415 the fifteen Swordfish aircraft detailed for the strike were ready in the hangar and the crews briefed. They were brought up on deck and at 1450 they began to take off. The pilots and observers had been led to expect a lone ship and fully impressed with the great importance of their mission, they were determined to press home their attack. One aircraft developed a defect on taking off and had to be re-embarked.

During the afternoon the *Rodney* was sighted from the *King George V* converging slowly on her from the port beam and by 1800 she had taken station astern of the flagship. Asked by the Commander-in-Chief what speed he could do, Captain Dalrymple-Hamilton optimistically replied, '22 knots', but this proved to be rather more than the seventeen-year-old ship, badly in need of a refit, could manage. The *Rodney* still had the destroyers *Tartar* and *Mashona* in company, the *Somali* having had to be detached to replenish with fuel. Although Admiral Tovey had been hoping for the arrival of Captain Vian's flotilla, he quite expected that on receipt of the position of the *Bismarck* he would have decided to disregard his previous instructions and lead his destroyers towards the enemy with a view to delivering a night torpedo attack. What the Commander-in-Chief was anxiously awaiting was the result of the strike by *Ark Royal*'s aircraft. Little did he know what mischance had attended it.

To reinforce the two shadowing Swordfish aircraft, and in view of the adverse state of the weather, at 1315 Admiral Somerville had ordered the cruiser *Sheffield* to proceed ahead and establish contact with the *Bismarck*. Unfortunately the message being transmitted visually was not received by the *Ark Royal* and being preoccupied with the operation of aircraft, the departure of the *Sheffield* in the prevailing poor visibility went unobserved. The Admiral followed up his plain language signal to the *Sheffield* with an encrypted one addressed to the Admiralty and repeated to the *Ark Royal*, stating what he had done but owing to the large number of messages being received at that time, especially those from the shadowing aircraft, and the fact that it was only repeated for information, there was some delay in decoding it. It was not, therefore, shown to Captain Maund until more than an hour after the strike had been launched, and when he read it he at once realised the disastrous consequences which might result from this lack of information. He immediately sent off a signal in plain language to the Striking Force, 'Look out for *Sheffield*' but alas, it was too late.

The *Sheffield* was aware of the despatch of the Striking Force and it was, therefore, no surprise to Captain Larcom, her commanding officer, when at about 1545 he sighted it and a warning went out to the A/A gun positions that friendly aircraft were approaching. The *Sheffield* was at the time about 20 miles to the north of the *Bismarck* but not yet in touch with her. Suddenly, to everyone's amazement they noticed that the aircraft had broken formation and were diving to the attack. Captain Larcom went on to full speed and put his helm hard over to confuse their aim, but a further surprise was in store. The warheads of half the torpedoes released exploded on hitting the water or in the wake, so that he only had to avoid the six or seven which did not explode, and this he successfully managed to do. Moreover, as a result of good fire discipline, not a shot had been fired.

When Admiral Tovey received Admiral Somerville's report of the result of the air strike which tersely announced 'No hits' he felt that the scales were now tilted very much in favour of the *Bismarck*. Even when he received the amplifying news that another strike would take off at 1830, the failure of the first one about which he had as yet received no details, did not augur well for the success of the second, which he appreciated would be the last one that day. There were still Captain Vian's destroyers and he knew that under his forceful leadership the attacks would be pressed well home, yet a single ship with complete freedom of manoeuvre was not an easy target and the prevailing weather could not have been more unfavourable for destroyer night torpedo attacks. Fuel in the *King George V* was now down to 32 per cent remaining and the *Rodney* had only enough to allow her to remain until 0800/27, so the unpleasant fact had to be faced that unless there was a favourable change in the situation during the night he would be obliged to abandon the chase. After four days and nights of pursuit covering over 2000 miles, it was a heartbreaking situation with which to be confronted.

A dispirited bunch of airmen returned to the *Ark Royal*, but Captain Maund soon restored their morale. He exonerated them from all blame for the mistake and told them they would have another opportunity to strike at the *Bismarck* as soon as their aircraft had been re-armed and re-fuelled. Further, that the obviously defective Duplex pistols fitted to the torpedoes would be replaced by contact ones set to run at 22 feet. Meanwhile, at 1740 the *Sheffield* had sighted the *Bismarck* and taken station ten miles astern of her from which position she was able to shadow her closely. *Ark Royal's* second striking force consisting of fifteen Swordfish, took off at 1910 and formed up in two squadrons of three sub-flights. The *Sheffield* had reported the enemy as bearing 167° distant 38 miles from the carrier and the aircraft had been ordered to get in touch with the cruiser so that she could use her D/F equipment to guide them to their target. As they neared the *Bismarck* they entered a bank of thick cloud, the base of which was only about 700 feet from the water. While climbing through it the force became split up, but at 2047 number one sub-flight of three aircraft to which one of number three sub-flight had attached itself, dived through the cloud to sight the *Bismarck* about four miles away down wind. They manoeuvred to approach her from the port beam and under intense and accurate fire, released their torpedoes, one of which was seen to hit. During the next forty minutes the remaining aircraft, some of which came upon the enemy from an unexpected direction and had either to work round or take cloud cover before making a fresh approach, made their attacks. The flak was intense and to the Germans it seemed that it was only the flimsy canvas structure of the aircraft through which the A/A shells tore without detonating that saved them from complete destruction. Altogether thirteen torpedoes were fired, two having been jettisoned, and two hits and one probable hit were claimed. All the aircraft returned safely though five had been damaged by gunfire and the pilot and gunner of one of them were wounded; one aircraft crash landed.

The real extent of the damage inflicted on the *Bismarck* was not at first apparent to the British forces. Lieutenant-Commander Gerhard Junack, an engineer officer and survivor from the *Bismarck*, describes it as follows:

'One torpedo which hit amidships caused no damage, but the second affected the rudders disastrously by jamming the portside rudder at a 15° angle. Immediately the *Bismarck* became no longer manoeuvrable. The torpedo hit on the rudder shook the ship so badly that even in my zone of action in the turbine room the deck plates were thrown in the air and the hull vibrated violently. . . . The stern compartments in the ship were now flooding, but the men who had been stationed there could still be saved and soon the carpenters and repair crew came through making their way aft . . . eventually it was found possible to connect the hand rudder. But the old rudder would not budge and to attempt to cut it away with underwater saws was quite impossible because of the heavy swell. A proposal to force the rudder out from below with the help of explosives was rejected because of the proximity to the propellers.'*

Admiral Lütjens seems quickly to have reached the conclusion that there was now little chance of saving the ship from the fate that he was certain would sooner or later overtake her. At 2140 he signalled Group West, 'Ship no longer manoeuvrable—we fight to the last shell—Long live the Führer'.

The *Sheffield* was the first to appreciate that something serious was amiss when she noticed that the *Bismarck* had veered round to port and she found herself under fire from her 15in guns. Six accurate salvoes were discharged and although no hits were obtained, splinters from a near miss killed three men and wounded two others stationed at the anti-aircraft guns. The cruiser made smoke and turned away at high speed and as she did so Captain Vian's destroyers were observed approaching from the westward and they were directed on to their target. At 2136 Captain Larcom reported that the *Bismarck* appeared to be steering 340° and four minutes later he amended it to North, then at about 2155 he lost touch and continued on what he believed was a parallel course to the stricken ship.

Admiral Tovey received the *Sheffield*'s reports of the *Bismarck*'s course with a certain amount of reserve, but at 2142 he altered course to south and steered towards her position with a view to making contact from the eastward. However, when at 2228 he received a signal from Admiral Somerville reporting that *Ark Royal*'s second strike had achieved a hit, followed twelve minutes later by a claim to have made a possible second one, he decided in view of the gather-

* *The Last Hours of the Bismarck* by Lieutenant-Commander Gerhard Junack, Purnell's History of the Second World War, Vol. 2, No. 5.

ing darkness and the uncertain prospects of interception under favourable conditions, to defer engagement until dawn. To that end, at 2306 he altered course to the eastward and northward to work his way around the *Bismarck* so as to approach her from the west when she would be silhouetted against the eastern horizon.

As Captain Vian, with his five destroyers spread two and a half miles apart on a line of bearing 070°–250°, swept downwind on a south-easterly course of 120° towards his target, he hoped to contact her ahead of his own ship, the *Cossack*, but instead the Polish destroyer *Piroun* on his port wing was the first to sight her. At 2228 she reported the *Bismarck* bearing 145° distant 9 miles. He had decided that now that the battleship was apparently disabled, his first duty was to shadow her and in every way assist the Commander-in-Chief in bringing her to action with his two battleships. At the same time he hoped that there would be opportunities for delivering torpedo attacks on her which would cripple her still further, provided these did not involve heavy losses to his ships. At 2248, therefore, he ordered his ships to take up shadowing positions all round the *Bismarck*. It took a little time for some of the destroyers to work round to their positions without getting too close to their still very formidable opponent. The *Piroun* quickly discovered the need for caution when at a range of 13500 yards she engaged her much larger opponent and received in reply three salvoes of 15in shells one of which straddled her. As darkness fell the weather appeared to deteriorate and the heavy rain squalls became more frequent, conditions which did not favour a synchronised torpedo attack. Nevertheless at 2324 Vian ordered his ships to take up stations for the delivery of one, but soon afterwards, realising how adverse the circumstances were, he cancelled the order and told them to attack independently.

Meanwhile on board the *Bismarck* all hope of freeing the damaged rudder appears to have been abandoned. At 2358 Admiral Lütjens despatched another heroic signal, this time addressed to Hitler, 'We fight to the last in our belief in you my Führer, and in the firm faith of Germany's victory', to which Hitler duly replied, and in a message to the crew promised, 'What can still be done, will be done', but apart from ordering all U-boats in the area to concentrate round her whether they had torpedoes or not, and having tugs stand by in case there should be a favourable change in the situation, little else was possible. She was still too far out for effective air support, the *Scharnhorst* and *Gneisenau* were unfit for sea, and the weather was too bad for destroyers of the much smaller type available. From 2300 onwards the *Bismarck* headed at slow speed into the wind, using her engines from time to time to alter course so as to open 'A' arcs or to avoid the torpedoes aimed at her by the destroyers, as first one, then another and occasionally in pairs, they closed in to deliver their attacks. Darkness, usually the cloak under which such attacks are made, now advantaged them not at all. The *Bismarck* greeted every attempt with accurately placed salvoes of both large and small calibre shell. At 2342 Captain Vian's ship, *Cossack*, was subjected to this treatment, while still 8000 yards away and splinters removed some of her radio aerials. The *Zulu* had a similar experience some eight minutes later, being straddled by three 15in salvoes; splinters from which wounded one officer and two ratings. The *Sikh* was shadowing from astern when at 0020 the *Bismarck* made a large alteration of course to port and opened fire on her, the shell splashes preventing the Torpedo control officer from taking aim, so she had to withdraw without attacking. The *Maori*, close on the *Sikh*'s port beam, endeavoured to take over her shadowing duty but the battle-ship again swung round and for a time succeeded in throwing off all the shadowing destroyers.

At 0100 the *Zulu* steering westward resighted the *Bismarck* right ahead so she increased to 25 knots and zigzagging to hinder her aim, ran up on her port quarter unobserved and at 0121 fired two tor-pedoes at a range of 5000 yards, immediately coming under heavy fire from the enemy who, during the approach had swung round from northwest to northeast and so the torpedoes missed. It was now the *Maori*'s turn. Her Captain, Commander H. T. Armstrong DSC, RN, an officer of great experience and intrepidity, observing that the enemy ship was now heading 040° crept up on her port quarter to within 4000 yards and apparently undetected. When he reached her beam he fired a star shell in order the better to illuminate her and noticed that she was turning to starboard, so at 0137 he fired two torpedoes one of which he believed was a hit. He then manoeuvred to deliver another attack from the starboard bow, but the *Bismarck* had by now opened a very heavy fire with her main, secondary and close-range weapons, so he was obliged to withdraw at full speed and although the enemy's fire followed him out to 10000 yards, providentially his ship escaped damage. Three minutes after the *Maori*'s attack Captain Vian who had been creeping up on the battleship from the northeast, fired three torpedoes at her from a range of 6000 yards. The target was plainly silhouetted in the flashes of her guns as she engaged the retiring *Maori*, and one certain torpedo hit was observed. Possibly, as a result of these hits the *Bismarck* appears to have stopped and was so reported by the *Zulu* at 0148. The *Sikh*, which at this time was closing in from the southward, decided to try and carry out an unseen attack. At 0218, her captain, Commander G. H. Stokes RN, having verified from his radar plot that the battleship was indeed stopped, fired four torpedoes from a range of 7000 yards and one hit was believed to have been made. Thereafter, he managed to keep in touch with the enemy until 0359.

Although the destroyers were making full and frequent reports of the *Bismarck*'s position and movements, they were not in sight of the Commander-in-Chief who was naturally anxious that any difference in reckoning between them and his flagship, HMS *King George V*, should be reconciled before contact was made, so at 0236 he ordered them to fire star shell at half-hourly intervals, but the frequent rain squalls often obscured them and the firing ships attracted so much attention from the enemy that Captain Vian had to order them to desist.

At about 0240 it appears that the *Bismarck* again got under way and proceeded slowly in a north-westerly direction. At 0225 the *Cossack* managed to deliver another attack on her with her one remaining torpedo at a range of 4000 yards but no hit was claimed and she came under heavy fire, so she withdrew to the northward under smoke and subsequently altered to the west.

Once again, at 0400, touch with the *Bismarck* was temporarily lost, but her position was by now known and her movements were so obviously restricted that regaining contact did not present any great problem. The position of the destroyers relative to her at this time was:

Cossack to the west-north-west, *Sikh*, *Zulu*, *Maori* and *Piorun* spread in the sector covering south-east to south-west and all were now moving in to regain touch.

In the event this does not appear to have been achieved until just before 0600. An hour previously Captain Vian had reluctantly detached the *Piorun* to return to Plymouth for fuel. Her captain, Commander Plawski, was longing to get in a torpedo attack but it was now getting light and it would have been an unnecessary risk to his ship and fine ship's company to have attempted one.

At 0550 the *Maori* resighted the *Bismarck* steering a mean course of 340° at 7 knots and at 0625 she illuminated her with star shell just as she emerged from a rain squall into full view of the *Sikh* who, however, got away without being engaged. Twenty minutes later the *Maori* fired two torpedoes at a range of about 9000 yards, both of which missed, but the *Bismarck* opened fire on her so she went on to 28 knots and withdrew without being hit. This was the last of the destroyer torpedo attacks and taking into account the bad weather, the way in which they had clung to the *Bismarck* and harassed her with torpedo fire without themselves suffering damage, although coming repeatedly under intense gunfire, was described by the Commander-in-Chief as 'a model of its kind'. The question of how many torpedo hits were obtained during these attacks will never be known with absolute certainty. The German account based mainly on survivors' stories, infers that none was obtained, and considering that the *Bismarck* was constantly changing course and speed it would not be in the least surprising if that were the case. The destroyers now took up positions all round the damaged German battleship from which they could watch and report her movements, and so deliver her at the appointed time to the approaching British battleships.

CHAPTER SIX

The Final Phase

As dawn broke on the morning of May 27 the avenging forces summoned by the Admiralty from far and wide were closing in for the final reckoning with the damaged but still formidable *Bismarck*. To the northward of her were the Commander-in-Chief with the *King George V* and *Rodney*, shortly to be joined by Rear-Admiral Wake-Walker in the *Norfolk*, whom we last heard of complying with Admiral Tovey's order to search to the eastward, but who since the enemy's relocation had been steering to the south-eastward first at 27 knots and later at 30 knots. When he intercepted the report of *Ark Royal's* aircraft success in torpedoing the *Bismarck* he altered course more to the southward and steered in the direction indicated by the flashes of star shell fired by the destroyers. His intention was to reach a position to the northward of the enemy from which he would be able to spot the fall of shot of the two battleships. He sighted the *Bismarck* at 0753/27, 9 miles away on a bearing of 145° and a quarter of an hour later the *King George V* loomed up 12 miles away to the southward so he was able to establish a visual link between them. Another 8in gun cruiser, the *Dorsetshire*, was escorting a homeward bound convoy from Sierra Leone when she intercepted the Catalina's sighting report of 1056/26. She was then some 360 miles south of the *Bismarck*, but leaving the auxiliary cruiser *Bulolo* in charge of the convoy, she shaped course at high speed to the northward. She soon ran into the area swept by the north-westerly gale and was obliged to reduce speed to 25 knots and later to 20 knots. At 0833/27 she sighted the *Cossack* ahead to whom she identified herself and who gave her the bearing and distance of the *Bismarck* as 290° 6 miles. She had reached the scene of action just in time, having covered 600 miles since leaving her convoy.

Admiral Somerville, who had instructed the *Ark Royal* to be ready to carry out a dawn air strike on the *Bismarck* with twelve Swordfish aircraft, had turned south at 0115/27 and a quarter of an hour later

61

the Commander-in-Chief instructed him to keep Force H not less than 20 miles south of the *Bismarck* so as to give the battleships a clear line of approach. At 0509 while it was still dark, an aircraft was flown off from *Ark Royal* to spot for the *King George V*'s guns, but in the gale force wind and cloud-laden sky, it failed to locate the *Bismarck* and was obliged to return. The dawn attack was also cancelled on account of the poor visibility since, with so many ships around he was anxious that there should be no repetition of the *Sheffield* incident which, but for good luck, might well have proved disastrous. At 0810, after receiving a report from the *Maori* which had been sighted to the northward, that the *Bismarck* was only 11 miles away from her and therefore 17 from the *Renown*, Admiral Somerville ordered his force to steer southwest to open its distance from the enemy.

Action

Although the north-westerly gale was blowing with undiminished force the light was good and the horizon clear to the northeastward as seen from the bridge of the *King George V*. Admiral Tovey decided that in the circumstances the weather gauge had distinct advantages, so he planned to approach the *Bismarck* from the west-north-west and if the enemy continued to head in that direction, to deploy to the southward and engage on opposite courses at about 15000 yards.

Between 0600 and 0700 on that fateful morning, the destroyer *Maori* acting as a link between the *King George V* and the *Bismarck*, prior to the arrival of the *Norfolk*, enabled the British battleship to obtain an accurate plot of the *Bismarck*'s position, course and speed which was of the greatest help in deciding on the course to steer to make contact. It appeared that the *Bismarck* was more or less steady on a course of 330° and making good a speed of about 10 knots. At 0708, in contrast to the rigid formation in which Vice-Admiral Holland had manoeuvred his two ships prior to action with the *Bismarck*, Admiral Tovey told the *Rodney* to assume open order (that is to increase her distance to 6 cables) and to adjust her bearing as suited her best. At 0737 the *King George V* led round to a course of 080° and the *Rodney* took station 20° before her port beam. At 0820, as previously mentioned, the *Norfolk* was sighted and as she was also

---

Diagram 6. (*Opposite*) Final action against *Bismarck* on May 27.

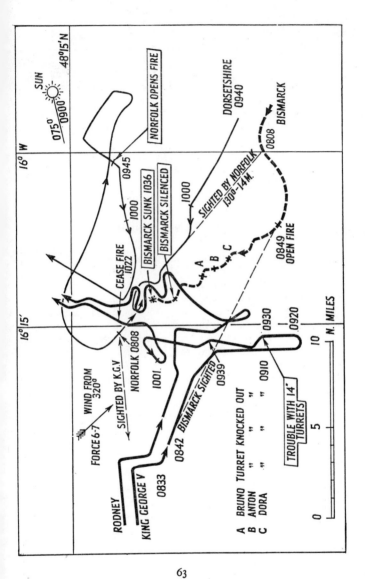

SUN 075° 0900

48°15'N

16° W

NORFOLK OPENS FIRE

DORSETSHIRE 0940

BISMARCK 0808

0945

1000

SIGHTED BY NORFOLK 1300-14 M.

1000

BISMARCK SUNK 1036

BISMARCK SILENCED

CEASE FIRE 1022

0849 OPEN FIRE

A B C

WIND FROM 320°

FORCE 6-7

SIGHTED BY K.G.V.

NORFOLK 0808

1001.

0930

0920

N. MILES

RODNEY

KING GEORGE V 0833

0842 BISMARCK SIGHTED

0939

0910

TROUBLE WITH 14" TURRETS

A BRUNO TURRET KNOCKED OUT
B ANTON " "
C DORA " "

0 5 10

63

in sight of the *Bismarck* she was able to take over the duties of 'visual link' up till then so successfully performed by the *Maori*. During the run in the Commander-in-Chief twice made adjustments to his line of approach and at 0843 the *Bismarck* came into view almost right ahead, bearing 118° distant 25000 yards. At the time the two British battleships were steering 110° in line abreast 8 cables apart.

The *Rodney* opened fire at 0847, followed a minute later by the *King George V*. An eye-witness in the latter ship described the event:

'There was a sort of crackling roar to port—the *Rodney* has opened fire with her 16in guns and an instant later the *King George V* lets fly with her 14in. I have my glasses on the *Bismarck*. She fires all four guns from her two forward turrets, four thin orange flames. The Germans have a reputation for hitting with their early salvos. Now I know what suspended animation means. It seems to take about two hours for those shots to fall!! The splashes shoot up opposite but beyond the *Rodney*'s foc'sle.'*

The *Bismarck* opened fire at 0850 and while her first salvo fell short, with her third and fourth she straddled the *Rodney* which, having freedom of manoeuvre, was able to take avoiding action by steering towards where the last salvo had fallen knowing that a range correction would be applied to the next one which would therefore, miss. At 0854 the *Norfolk* joined in the action with her 8in guns from her position on the enemy's starboard bow at a range of about 22000 yards. Five minutes later, when the range was down to 16000 yards, the *King George V* swung round to starboard to open her 'A' arcs. The *Rodney*, which had been steering an opening course from the flagship, conformed a few minutes later but by now the distance between them was about $2\frac{1}{2}$ miles. With the wind on the starboard quarter there was considerable interference from cordite smoke and funnel gases so that spotting the fall of shot became very difficult. The problem was overcome to some extent with the help of radar. Soon after the *King George V* turned south, the *Bismarck* turned north and shifted her fire to her, and it became an engagement on opposite courses. The eye-witness onboard the *King George V* comments:

'The *Bismarck* turned north, steaming about 12 or 14 knots. We kept turning in and out to confuse the enemy range-takers, all the while closing the range rapidly. The Admiral kept on saying

* Quoted by F. McMurtrie in *The Cruise of the Bismarck*, p. 32.

"Close the range; get closer, get close—I can't see enough hits" and so we closed the range.'*

At 0902 a shell or shells from the *Rodney* were seen to hit the *Bismarck* forward and it appeared that her forward turrets had been put out of action. This is supported by Lieutenant-Commander Junack who has written:

'Shortly after the battle commenced a shell hit the combat mast and the fire control post in the foremast broke away. At 0902 both forward heavy gun turrets were put out of action. A further hit wrecked the forward control post, the rear control post was wrecked soon after—and that was the end of the fighting instruments.'†

At 0904 the *Dorsetshire* on the *Bismarck*'s starboard quarter, opened fire at a range of 20000 yards so she was now under attack from all sides. The number of shell splashes falling around her increased the difficulty of observing the fall of shot, and after nine minutes the *Dorsetshire* checked fire. The range between the *King George V* and the *Bismarck* was now steady at about 12000 yards and at 0905 the former's secondary battery of 5·25in guns opened fire, but they added to the interference caused by cordite smoke and after two or three minutes they were ordered to cease fire. Meanwhile, the *Rodney* fired six of her 24·5in torpedoes at the enemy at an estimated range of 11000 yards and the *Norfolk* four 21in torpedoes at an estimated range of 16000 yards, but none of them scored a hit.

The *Bismarck*'s bearing from both the *King George V* and the *Rodney* was drawing rapidly aft, and at 0916 Captain Dalrymple-Hamilton turned his ship 180° to starboard, but when the turn was completed he was only 8600 yards from the enemy and at that range the effect of his 16in guns was truly devastating. The *King George V* did not turn until nine minutes later and Captain Patterson turned 150° to port, which put him 12000 yards from the *Bismarck*. Things were not going too well in the *King George V*. Being to leeward her view of the target was obscured by smoke and the splashes of the *Rodney*'s shells and her gunnery radar set had temporarily broken down. Further, her 14in gun turrets were suffering from the same kind of mechanical defects which had afflicted those in the *Prince of Wales*. One of them was out of action for half an hour and two

* McMurtrie, *ibid.*
† Junack, *ibid.*

others for shorter periods, so that for seven minutes her fire power was reduced by 80 per cent and for twenty-three minutes by 40 per cent and this, in less favourable circumstances, might have had very serious consequences. At 1005 she closed the *Bismarck* to about 3000 yards and fired several salvoes at this point blank range, then she resumed her northerly course.

The *Bismarck*'s after guns, now firing in local control, shifted their fire from the *King George V* to the *Rodney* and several shots fell close, one damaging the sluice door of her starboard underwater torpedo tube into which a torpedo had just been loaded. The turn to the north and into the wind had cleared the range and it was now possible to see the damage being inflicted on the *Bismarck*. The same eye-witness has recorded:

> 'About this time, the coppery glow of our secondary armament shells striking the armoured upper works became more and more frequent, and one fierce flame shot up from the base of the bridge structure, enveloping it as high as and including the spotting top for a flickering second.'[*]

About this time the *Bismarck* appeared to slow down and the *Rodney* began to overhaul her. Zigzagging across her bows she continued to pour a shattering fire into the blazing and battered hull of the German ship. She fired another four torpedoes at her, but again without success. Most of the *Bismarck*'s guns had been silenced, only the after superimposed turret and a few of the secondary armament guns remained in action, but by 1010 even these had fallen silent. The *Bismarck* had fought a gallant fight but the odds against her were too great. Lieutenant-Commander Junack takes up the story:

> 'Gradually the noise of combat became more irregular until it sank, to become nothing more than a series of sporadic crashes; even the control bells from the bridge stopped ringing. All three turbine rooms were filled with smoke from the boiler room; fortunately no shells had yet come through the plating protecting the engineroom or the electric generators. . . . Somewhere about 1015 hours I received an order over the telephone from the Chief Engineer: "Prepare the ship for sinking". That was the last order I received on *Bismarck*. After that all transmission of orders collapsed.'[†]

[*] McMurtrie, *ibid*.
[†] Junack, *ibid*.

Other survivors have told of the fearful damage within the ship. Hatches and doors wrenched from their hinges littered the decks. The red glow of fires illumined the darkened passages and thick smoke and fumes from bursting shells poisoned the atmosphere and poured from great holes six feet wide blasted in the upper deck. Listing to port and wallowing in the trough of the Atlantic swell, the once pride of the German navy was now a black and burning hulk. But despite the terrible battering she had received, the *Bismarck* did not sink, much to Admiral Tovey's surprise. It seemed clear that further gunfire would not hasten her end, and both his ships being extremely short of fuel, at 1015 he ordered the *King George V* and *Rodney* to break off the action and steer 027°. At 1036 he directed the *Dorsetshire* to finish her off with torpedoes, but meanwhile the fuses of the scuttling charges had been lit. At 1010 the *Norfolk*, after waiting for the *King George V* and the *Rodney* to move out of range, fired four torpedoes at a range of 4000 yards and although she claimed two hits it does not appear that any were obtained. Ten minutes later the *Dorsetshire*, approaching from the southward, fired two torpedoes one of which exploded under the bridge on the starboard side and the other further aft. She then circled round the *Bismarck*'s bows and at 1036 fired another torpedo from a range of 2600 yards into her port side, after which the great ship heeled over to port and started to sink by the stern; then she turned over and at 1040 disappeared from view.

There has been a great deal of discussion on the subject of whether the *Bismarck* sank as the result of the torpedo hits she had received, or the firing of the scuttling charges, or a combination of both. In the light of our present knowledge it seems reasonable to discount all the claims of torpedo hits other than those listed below, which show that she received six hits, three from 18in aircraft torpedoes and three from 21in torpedoes, viz: *Victorious*' aircraft, one starboard side, *Ark Royal*'s aircraft, one port side and one starboard side aft, *Dorsetshire* two starboard side and one port side. Except for the vital hit that damaged the rudder, it is quite possible that the other 18in torpedoes did little damage, if any. So only the effect of the *Dorsetshire*'s three torpedoes is in question. Herr Brennecke, who has clearly made a very detailed study of the subject has this to say:

'Did the battleship sink as a result of the torpedo hits or on account of the scuttling charges? According to the report of the *Dorsetshire* the two first torpedoes which hit the starboard side of the *Bismarck* from close range had no visible effect. A further torpedo which was fired by the heavy cruiser against the port side was said to have caused the end. Contrary to this are the reports of eye-witnesses who did not see any results of the torpedo hits when the ship overturned. In fact the expert and responsible shipbuilder of the *Bismarck* class says that the torpedo bulkheads were strong enough to withstand the impact of several torpedo hits. It is, however, possible in the case of the third torpedo that the water which had entered the lower compartments in the meantime as a result of the scuttling, so lessened the stability of the hull and of the torpedo protection devices that the *Bismarck* sank.'

He goes on to say:

'The question whether the heavily damaged battleship would have sunk without the scuttling charges and only on account of the torpedo hits cannot be positively answered. More probable, though not wholly provable, is the other theory that the torpedo hits had absolutely no effect and that the end of the *Bismarck* was entirely due to the scuttling measures undertaken.'*

It is difficult to believe that a torpedo exploding against the hull of a ship, even one as well built as was the *Bismarck*, would have no visible effect even though it might not injure the ship's watertight integrity, but in view of the fact that the *Dorsetshire*'s third and last torpedo was not fired until about fifteen minutes after the scuttling charges had been blown, it seems highly probable that the effect of this explosion on the already sinking ship was to hasten her end.

In his despatch on the action, Admiral Tovey paid a fitting tribute:

'The *Bismarck* had put up a most gallant fight against impossible odds, worthy of the old days of the Imperial German Navy, and she went down with her colours flying.'†

The *Dorsetshire* being the nearest to the scene of the sinking, signalled one of *Ark Royal*'s aircraft circling round to carry out an anti-submarine patrol round her while she stopped to rescue survivors

---

* Brennecke, *ibid.*, p. 230.
† *Bismarck, The Sinking of.* Supplement to the London Gazette No 38098 dated 16.10.1947.

in which task she was assisted by the *Maori*. The cruiser had picked up about 80 men under very difficult conditions with the ship rolling heavily in the sea and swell, when a suspicious smoky discharge was observed about two miles to leeward. Thinking it might indicate the presence of a U-boat she reluctantly got under way, leaving the *Maori* to do what she could for the remainder. Between them they rescued four officers and 110 men and later that evening submarine U-75 rescued a further three men, while the following night the German fishing vessel *Sachsenwald*, acting as a weather ship out of Bordeaux, picked up another two. The Spanish cruiser *Canarias* also hurried to the scene, but found only floating corpses. Thus, out of a ship's company of some 2400 only 119 were saved.

The anxiety about the presence of U-boats was fully justified as was subsequently discovered. U-556 had been ordered to rendezvous with the *Bismarck* and take off her war diary which, however, she did not succeed in doing. A month later she was sunk and it was learned from survivors that at 2100 on May 26 she had found herself within range of the *Renown* and *Ark Royal* with the latter on a steady course operating aircraft. She had, however, expended all her torpedoes and was therefore, unable to attack them. The German account of the operation also says:

'. . . the possibilities of supporting the *Bismarck* were limited to the determined efforts of the Air Force and the submarines available in the Biscay area. All the submarines in question, with or without torpedoes, were sent to the supposed position of the *Bismarck*.'*

On retiring to the northward the *King George V* and the *Rodney* were joined by the *Cossack*, *Sikh* and *Zulu* and by 1600 on the following day by eleven more destroyers despatched by the Admiralty to form an anti-submarine screen for the two battleships. Although it was fully expected that the Germans would retaliate for the sinking of the *Bismarck* by mounting a heavy air attack against them whilst they remained within range of the French airfields, in the event only four aircraft succeeded in locating them, one of which attacked one of the ships on the screen, and another jettisoned its bombs when attacked by a Blenheim fighter covering the fleet. The Commander-in-Chief with his force reached Loch Ewe safely at 1230 on May 29. Two of Captain Vian's flotilla, the *Tartar* and the *Mashona*, both of which were very short of fuel and, as a result, had been unable to

* Führer Naval Conference.

keep up with the rest of the fleet and had fallen about 100 miles astern, were not so lucky. At 0955/28 they were attacked by a strong force of enemy bombers sent out to attack the battleships. The two vessels stoutly fought off their attackers and tried to dodge the bombs aimed at them, but the *Mashona* was hit and began to settle. During a lull, the *Tartar* stopped and took off her crew, but she remained under attack for the rest of the day. Late that afternoon she was joined by two destroyers detached by Admiral Tovey, and all three ships reached port safely the next day. The losses in the *Mashona* amounted to one officer and 45 men.

The Commander-in-Chief's Views on the Action

Altogether five battleships, three battle-cruisers, two aircraft carriers, four heavy and seven light cruisers and twenty-one destroyers in addition to some fifty aircraft from Coastal Command were employed in the operations leading up to the sinking of the *Bismarck* in what was one of the most dramatic episodes of World War II. It provided an excellent example of the use of sea-air or maritime power in which both shore-based and sea-borne aircraft played a decisive part. The German ship's lack of air support proved her undoing, as Raeder well knew it might. In a well deserved tribute to the British forces taking part, Admiral Sir John Tovey wrote:

'Although it was no more than I expected, the co-operation, skill and understanding displayed by all forces during this prolonged chase gave me the utmost satisfaction. Flag and Commanding Officers of detached units invariably took the action I would have wished, before or without receiving instructions from me. The conduct of all officers and men of the Fleet which I have the honour to command was in accordance with the tradition of the Service. Force H was handled with conspicuous skill throughout the operation by Vice-Admiral Sir James F. Somerville KCB, DSO and contributed a vital share in its successful conclusion. The accuracy of the enemy information supplied by the Admiralty and the speed with which it was passed were remarkable and the balance struck between information and instructions passed to forces out of visual touch with me was ideal.'*

The valuable part played by Coastal Command was recognised in a message sent by the Admiralty to its Commander-in-Chief:

* Official despatch, paras. 92 and 93, London Gazette No 38098.

'The Admiralty wish gratefully to acknowledge the part played by the reconnaissance forces under your command which contributed in a large measure to the successful outcome of the recent operations.'

Movements of the Prinz Eugen

Nothing more was heard of the *Prinz Eugen* from the time she parted company with the *Bismarck* at about 1800 on May 24 until June 4 when she was reported to have arrived at Brest. After being detached, Captain Brinkmann's first thought was to replenish with fuel from one of the supply ships which had been provided for the purpose. He accordingly steered to make contact with the tankers *Spickern* and *Esso Hamburg* which had been stationed 400 miles west and 450 miles northwest of Fayal in the Azores, respectively. He contacted the *Spickern* at 0906 on May 26 and refuelled from her. Two reconnaissance ships, the *Gonzenheim* and the *Kota Pinang*, originally stationed 300 miles south of Cape Farewell, Greenland, had been placed at his disposal and late on May 27 he made a rendezvous with them and the following day he topped up with fuel from the *Esso Hamburg*. He intended to move further south and carry out cruiser warfare in the area to the north and west of the Cape Verde Islands but on the 29th his Chief Engineer informed him that an inspection of the main engines indicated that an extensive overhaul was necessary, so he abandoned his plan and decided to make for Brest at his best speed, reaching there on June 1 having covered 7000 miles at an average speed of 24 knots. Her arrival marked the end of Operation Rheinübung and with it all hopes of the use of German surface ships in the war against shipping. Raeder records:

'The loss of the *Bismarck* had a decisive effect on the conduct of the war at sea. Hitler's attitude to my proposals now changed too. Up to then he had left me more or less a free hand. . . . But now he became much more critical and more inclined to insist on his own views than before. . . . Now his instructions to me circumscribed my use of such heavy units.'*

On the debit side too had to be added the loss of all the supply ships and reconnaissance vessels supporting the operation. By the middle of June they had all either been scuttled or were sunk by ships of the British fleet.

* Raeder, *ibid.*, p. 214.

PART TWO

List of Flag and Commanding Officers and Ships Taking Part in Operations Against the Bismarck

Name of Ship	Type*	Flag and/or Commanding Officer	Initial Disposition
King George V	B	Flag of Admiral Sir John Tovey Commander-in-Chief, Home Fleet Captain W. R. Patterson CVO, RN	Scapa
Rodney	B	Captain F. H. G. Dalrymple-Hamilton RN	At Sea
Repulse	BC	Captain W. C. Tennant CB, CVO, RN	Clyde
Hood	BC	Flag of Vice-Admiral L. E. Holland CB Captain R. Kerr CBE, RN	Scapa
Prince of Wales	B	Captain J. C. Leach MVO, RN	Scapa
Victorious	AC	Captain H. C. Bovell RN	Scapa
Norfolk	C	Flag of Rear-Admiral W. F. Wake-Walker CB Captain A. J. L. Phillips RN	Denmark Strs
Suffolk	C	Captain R. M. Ellis RN	Denmark Strs
Galatea	C	Flag of Rear-Admiral A. T. B. Curteis CB Captain E. W. B. Sim RN	Scapa

* AC=Aircraft Carrier, B=Battleship, BC=Battle-cruiser, C=Cruiser, D=Destroyer, S/M=Submarine.

Name of Ship	Type	Flag and/or Commanding Officer	Initial Disposition
Aurora	C	Captain W. G. Agnew RN	Scapa
Kenya	C	Captain M. M. Denny CB, RN	Scapa
Neptune	C	Captain R. C. O'Conor RN	Scapa
Arethusa	C	Captain A. C. Chapman RN	At Sea
Edinburgh	C	Commodore C. M. Blackman DSO, RN	At Sea
Manchester	C	Captain H. A. Packer RN	Iceland–Faroes Passage
Birmingham	C	Captain A. C. G. Madden RN	
Inglefield	D	Captain P. Todd DSO, RN	Scapa
Active	D	Lieut-Commander M. W. Tomkinson RN	Scapa
Antelope	D	Lieut-Commander R. B. N. Hicks RN	Scapa
Achates	D	Lieut-Commander Viscount Jocelyn RN	Scapa
Anthony	D	Lieut-Commander J. M. Hodges RN	Scapa
Electra	D	Commander C. W. May RN	Scapa
Echo	D	Lieut-Commander C. H. de B. Newby RN	Scapa
Somali	D	Captain C. Caslon RN	At Sea with
Tartar	D	Commander L. P. Skipwith RN	HMS
Mashona	D	Commander W. H. Selby RN	*Rodney*
Eskimo	D	Lieutenant J. V. Wilkinson RN	
Punjabi	D	Commander S. A. Buss MVO, RN	Scapa
Intrepid	D	Commander R. C. Gordon DSO, RN	Scapa
Icarus	D	Lieut-Commander D. C. Maud DSC, RN	Scapa
Nestor	D	Commander C. B. Alers-Hankey DSC, RN	Scapa
Jupiter	D	Lieut-Commander N. V. J. T. Thew RN	London-derry

Western Approaches Command

Hermione	C	Captain G. N. Oliver RN	Scapa

Name of Ship	Type	Flag and/or Commanding Officer	Initial Disposition
Lance	D	Lieut-Commander R. W. F. Northcott RN	Scapa
Legion	D	Commander R. F. Jessel RN	Clyde as escort for HMS *Repulse*
Saguenay	D	Commander G. R. Miles RCN	
Assiniboine	D	Commodore G. C. Jones RCN	
Columbia	D	Lieut-Commander S. W. Davis RN	London-derry

Plymouth Command

Name of Ship	Type	Flag and/or Commanding Officer	Initial Disposition
Cossack	D	Captain P. L. Vian DSO, RN	Clyde as escort for Convoy WS.8B
Sikh	D	Commander G. H. Stokes RN	
Zulu	D	Commander H. R. Graham DSO, RN	
Maori	D	Commander H. T. Armstrong DSC, RN	
Piorun	D	Commander E. Plawski, Polish Navy	

Nore Command

Name of Ship	Type	Flag and/or Commanding Officer	Initial Disposition
Windsor	D	Lieut-Commander Hon. J. M. G. Waldegrave DSC, RN	Scapa

Force H

Name of Ship	Type	Flag and/or Commanding Officer	Initial Disposition
Renown	BC	Flag of Vice-Admiral Sir James F. Somerville KCB, DSO Captain R. R. McGrigor RN	Gibraltar
Ark Royal	AC	Captain L. E. Maund RN	Gibraltar
Sheffield	C	Captain C. A. A. Larcom RN	Gibraltar
Faulknor	D	Captain A. F. de Salis RN	Gibraltar
Foresight	D	Commander J. S. C. Salter RN	Gibraltar
Forester	D	Lieut-Commander E. B. Tancock RN	Gibraltar
Foxhound	D	Commander G. H. Peters DSC, RN	Gibraltar
Fury	D	Lieut-Commander T. C. Robinson RN	Gibraltar
Hesperus	D	Lieut-Commander A. A. Tait RN	Gibraltar

Name of Ship	Type	Flag and/or Commanding Officer	Initial Disposition
America and West Indies Command			
Ramillies	B	Captain A. D. Read RN	At Sea
Revenge	B	Captain E. R. Archer RN	Halifax NS
South Atlantic Command			
Dorsetshire	C	Captain B. C. S. Martin RN	At Sea
Submarines			
Minerve	S/M	Lieut de Vaisseau P. M. Sommerville FFN	On patrol off SW Norway
P31	S/M	Lieut J. B. de B. Kershaw RN	Scapa
Sealion	S/M	Commander B. Bryant DSC, RN	English Channel
Seawolf	S/M	Lieut P. L. Field RN	English Channel
Sturgeon	S/M	Lieut-Commander D. St Clair Ford RN	English Channel
Pandora	S/M	Lieut-Commander J. W. Linton RN	On passage Gibraltar to UK
Tigris	S/M	Lieut-Commander H. F. Bone DSO, DSC, RN	Clyde
H44	S/M	Lieut W. N. R. Knox DSC, RN	Rothesay

APPENDIX II

Ship's Data (British)

HMS King George V and Prince of Wales (Battleships)
Displacement: 38000 tons standard, 44460 tons full load.
Dimensions: length 700ft (213m) pp; beam 103ft (31·4m).
Draught: 27¾ft (8·4m).
Propulsion: 8 Admiralty Type boilers. Geared turbines. 4 shafts. SHP 125000.
Speed: 29 knots

Armament: Ten 14in (356mm) guns (2× 4) and (1× 2). Sixteen 5·25in (133mm) DP guns (8× 2). Forty-eight 2pdr A/A guns (6× 8). Sixteen 20mm single A/A guns.

Protection: 5½in (138mm) forward, 15in (381mm) abreast the magazines, 14in (356mm) abreast machinery spaces, 4½in (115mm) aft. 14in turrets—16in (406mm) face, 15in (381mm) sides, 9in (229mm) roof, 5·25in turrets—6in (152mm). Director Control tower and Barbettes 16in (406mm). Deck 1in (25mm) forward and aft, 6in (152mm) over magazines, 5in (127mm) over machinery spaces.

Radar: Type 281B—3m set used for long range A/A warning and range finding for aircraft and main armament. Type 282—50cm set for close range A/A guns. Type 284—50cm rangefinding set. Type 285—fitted to A/A directors of 5·25in guns.

Complement: 1640 private ship.

Builders: Vickers Armstrong—*King George V.* Cammell Laird—*Prince of Wales.*

HMS Hood (Battle-cruiser)

Displacement: 42462 tons standard, 48360 tons full load.

Dimensions: length 860ft (262m) pp; beam 105ft (32m).

Draught: 28½ft designed (8·6m), but in 1940 31½ft (9·5m).

Propulsion: Admiralty type boilers. Geared turbines. 4 shafts. SHP 144000.

Speed: designed 32 knots, in 1940 29½ knots.

Armament: Eight 15in (381cm) guns (4× 2). Twelve 5·5in (140mm) guns six each side. Eight 4in (100mm) A/A guns (4× 2). Twenty-four 2pdr (40mm) (3× 8). Four 21in (533mm) torpedoes in twin above water mountings. UP projectiles.

Protection: Main belt 5in (12·7cm) forward, 12in (30·5cm) amidships, 6in (15·2cm) aft, extending 9½ft (2·9m) below main deck. A strake of 7in (17·8cm) above the main belt reached to the upper deck, which was 1½in (3·7cm) thick. The main deck was 3in (7·6cm) thick and the lower deck 2in (5·1cm) thick.

Radar: There are no records to show with what radar sets the ship was equipped, but reliable sources indicate that she was fitted with Type 284 Gunnery radar only.

Complement: 1421 as flagship.

Builders: John Brown and Co, Clydebank.

HMS Rodney (Battleship)

Displacement: 33900 tons standard.

Dimensions: length 690ft (210m), beam 106ft (32·3m).

Draught: 28½ft (8·6m).

Propulsion: Geared turbines. 2 shafts. SHP 45000.

Speed: designed 23 knots, but in 1941 about 21 knots.

Armament: Nine 16in (406mm) guns (3 × 3). Twelve 6in (152mm) guns (6 × 2). Six 4·7in (120mm) A/A guns (6 × 1). *Twenty-four 2pdr (40mm) A/A guns (3 × 8). Two 24·5in (622mm) torpedo tubes below water.

Protection: Main belt 14in (35·6cm) over magazines and machinery spaces. Deck 3¾in (96mm) forward, 6¼in (165mm) over magazines and machinery. 16in turrets front and sides 16in (40·6cm), roof 9in (22·9)cm. Direct or Control tower and Barbettes 16in (40·6cm).

Radar: Type 281—3m set, air warning and surface ranging. Type 284 —50cm rangefinding set.

Complement: 1314.

Builder: Cammell Laird.

HMS Ramillies and Revenge (Battleships)

Displacement: 29150 tons standard.

Dimensions: length 580ft (176m) pp; 620½ft (189m) oa; beam 88½ft (27m) with bulges 102ft (31m).

Draught: 28½ft (8·6m).

Propulsion: Turbines. 4 shafts. SHP 40000.

Speed: 21½ knots.

Armament: Eight 15in (380mm) guns (4 × 2). Twelve 6in (150mm) guns (12 × 1). Eight 4in (102mm) A/A guns (4 × 2). Sixteen 2pdr A/A (2 × 8). *Revenge* 2 and *Ramillies* 4—21in (533mm) torpedoes STT.

Protection: Main belt 4–6in (102–152mm) at ends, 6–13in (152–330mm) amidships. Deck forward 1–2½in (25–63mm), amidships 1¾–2in (36–51mm), aft 3–5½in (76–139mm). Turrets sides 13in (330mm), roof 4¼in (108mm). Conning Tower 11–13in (279–330mm).

Complement: 1146.

Builders: Vickers Armstrong launched 29.5.15—*Revenge*. Beardmore launched 12.9.16—*Ramillies.*

HMS Renown (Battle-cruiser)

Displacement: 32000 tons standard.

Dimensions: length 750ft (228m) pp; beam 103ft (31·4m).

Draught: 27ft (8·2m).

Propulsion: Geared turbines. 4 shafts. SHP 120000.

Speed: 29 knots.

Armament: Six 15in (380mm) guns (3 × 2). Twenty 4·5in (115mm) DP guns (10 × 2). Twenty-four 2pdr (40mm) A/A guns (3 × 8).

Protection: Main belt 4–6in (10–15cm) forward, 6–9in (15–23cm) amidships, 3in (7·6cm) aft. Deck 2½–3in (6·3–7·6cm) forward, 3–4in

* Not fitted until after the action on May 26.

(7·6–10·2cm) amidships, 3½–4in (8·8–10·2cm) aft. Turrets 11in (28cm) sides, 9in (23cm) roof. Conning Tower 10in (25·4cm).
Aircraft: Two Walrus amphibians.
Complement: 1205.
Builders: Fairfields. Reconstructed and re-engined by Cammell Laird.

HMS Repulse (Battle-cruiser)
Displacement: 32000 tons standard.
Dimensions: length 750ft (228m) pp; beam 103ft (31·4m).
Draught: 27ft (8·2m).
Propulsion: Geared turbines. 4 shafts. SHP 120000.
Speed: 29 knots.
Armament: Six 15in (380mm) guns (3× 2). Twelve 4in (10·2cm) guns (4× 3). Eight 4in (10·2cm) A/A guns (2× 2) and (4× 1). Sixteen 2pdr (40mm) A/A guns (2× 8). Eight 21in (533mm) above water torpedo tubes.
Protection: Main belt 4–6in (10–15cm) forward, 6–9in (15–23cm) amidships, 3in (7·6cm) aft. Deck 2½–3in (6·3–7·6cm) forward, 3–4in (7·6–10·2cm) amidships, 3½–4in (8·8–10·2cm) aft. Turrets 11in (28cm) sides, 9in (23cm) roof, Conning Tower 10in (25·4cm).
Complement: 1181.
Builders: John Brown Ltd.

HMS Victorious (Aircraft carrier)
Displacement: 26000 tons standard.
Dimensions: length 673ft (205m) pp, 753ft (229m) oa; beam 95¾ft (29m).
Draught: 24ft (7·3m).
Propulsion: Geared turbines. 3 shafts. SHP 110000.
Speed: 32 knots.
Protection: Main belt and hangar sides 4½in (11·4cm). Flight deck 2½–3in (6·3–7·6cm).
Armament: Sixteen 4·5in (11·5cm) guns DP (8× 2). Forty-eight 2pdr (40mm) A/A guns (6× 8). Eight 20mm A/A guns (8× 1).
Aircraft: 72.
Complement: 1392.
Builders: Vickers Armstrong.

HMS Ark Royal (Aircraft carrier)
Displacement: 22000 tons standard.
Dimensions: length 685ft (209m) pp, 800ft (244m) oa; beam 94¾ft (28·8m).
Draught: 22¾ft (6·9m).
Propulsion: Geared turbines. 3 shafts. SHP 102000.

Speed: 30¾ knots.
Protection: Main belt 4½in (11·5cm). Flight deck 2½–3in (6·3–7·6cm).
Armament: Sixteen 4·5in (11·5cm) A/A guns (8 × 2). Forty-eight 2pdr
A/A (6 × 8). Eight 20mm A/A guns (8 × 1).
Aircraft: 72.
Complement: 1575.
Builders: Cammell Laird Ltd, launched 13.4.37.

HMS Norfolk and Dorsetshire (Cruisers)

Displacement: 9925 tons standard.
Dimensions: length 590ft (179m) pp, 630ft (192m) oa; beam 66ft (20m).
Draught: 17ft (5·2m).
Propulsion: Geared turbines. 4 shafts. SHP 80000.
Speed: 32 knots.
Armament: Eight 8in (203mm) guns (4 × 2). Eight 4in (102mm) A/A
guns (4 × 2). Sixteen 2pdr A/A guns (2 × 8). Eight 21in (533mm)
torpedoes AWTT.
Protection: Main belt 3–5in (76–127mm). Deck 1½–4in (38–102mm).
Turrets 1½–2in (38–51mm). DCT 3in (76mm).
Complement: 710 as flagship otherwise 679.
Builders: Fairfield launched 12.12.28—*Norfolk*. Portsmouth Dockyard
launched 29.1.29—*Dorsetshire*.

HMS Suffolk (Cruiser)

Displacement: 9800 tons standard.
Dimensions: length 590ft (179m) pp, 630ft (192m) oa; beam 68¼ft
(20·7m).
Draught: 16¼ft (4·9m).
Propulsion: Geared turbines. 4 shafts. SHP 80000.
Speed: 31½ knots.
Armament: Eight 8in (203mm) guns (4 × 2). Eight 4in (102mm) A/A
guns (4 × 2). Eight 2pdr A/A guns (2 × 4). Four 21in (533mm)
torpedoes AWTT.
Protection: Main belt 3–5in (76–127mm). Deck 1½in (38mm). Turrets
1½–2in (38–51mm). DCT 3in (76mm).
Complement: 710 a flagship otherwise 679.
Builders: Portsmouth Dockyard launched 16.2.26.
Note. Norfolk was fitted with Type 286 P radar which was a 1½m set
with two fixed aerials.
Suffolk was fitted with Types 279 and 284 radar, the former a 1½m
air warning set with a rotative aerial, the latter a 50cm rangefinding
set for main armament direction.

HMS Birmingham and Sheffield (Cruisers)

Displacement: 9100 tons.

Dimensions: length 591½ft (179·5m) oa, 558ft (170m) pp; beam 61¾ft (18·8m).
Draught: 17ft (5·2m).
Propulsion: Geared turbines. 4 shafts. SHP 75000.
Speed: 32 knots.
Armament: Twelve 6in (152mm) guns (4×3). Eight 4in (102mm) A/A guns (4×2). Eight 2pdr A/A guns (2×4). Eight 40mm A/A (4×2). Six 21in (533mm) torpedoes (2×3) AWTT.
Protection: Main belt 3–4in (76–102mm). Deck 2in (51mm). Turrets 1–2in (25·5–51mm). DCT 4in (102mm).
Aircraft: Three.
Complement: 700.
Builders: Devonport Dockyard launched 1.9.36—*Birmingham*. Vickers Armstrong launched 23.7.36—*Sheffield*.

HMS Manchester (Cruiser)
Displacement: 9400 tons.
Dimensions: length 558ft (170m) pp, 591½ft (179·5m) oa; beam 62¼ft (19m).
Draught: 17½ft (5·3m).
Propulsion: Geared turbines. 4 shafts. SHP 82500.
Speed: 32½ knots.
Armament: Twelve 6in (152mm) guns (4×3). Eight 4in (102mm) A/A guns (4×2). Eight 2pdr A/A guns (2×4). Eight 40mm A/A (4×2). Six 21in (533mm) torpedoes (2×3) AWTT.
Protection: Main belt 3–4in (76–102mm). Deck 2in (51mm). Turrets 1–2in (25·5–51mm). DCT 4in (102mm).
Aircraft: Three.
Complement: 700.
Builders: Hawthorne Leslie launched 12.4.37.

HMS Edinburgh (Cruiser)
Displacement: 10000 tons.
Dimensions: length 579ft (176m) pp, 613½ft (187m) oa; beam 63¼ft (19·3m).
Draught: 17¾ft (5·2m).
Propulsion: Geared turbines. 4 shafts. SHP 80000.
Speed: 32 knots.
Armament: Twelve 6in (152mm) guns (4×3). Twelve 4in (102mm A/A guns (6×2). Sixteen 2pdr A/A (2×8). Six 21in (533mm) torpedoes AWTT (2×3).
Protection: Main belt 4½in (115mm). Deck 2in (51mm). Turrets 2½–1in (64–25mm). DCT 4in (102mm).
Aircraft: Three.

Complement: 850.
Builder: Swan Hunter launched 31.3.38.

HMS Arethusa, Aurora and Galatea (Cruisers)

Displacement: 5220 tons standard.
Dimensions: length 480ft (146m) pp, 506ft (154m) oa; beam 51ft
 (16.2m).
Draught: 13¾ft (4m).
Propulsion: Geared turbines. 4 shafts. SHP 64000.
Speed: 32 knots.
Armament: Six 6in (152mm) guns (3×2). Eight 4in (102mm) A/A
 guns (4×2). Eight 2pdr A/A guns (2×4). Six 21in (533m) torpedoes
 (2×3) AWTT.
Protection: Main belt 2in (51mm). Deck 2in (51mm). Turrets and
 DCT 1in (25mm).
Complement: 450.
Builders: Chatham Dockyard launched 6.3.34—*Arethusa*. Portsmouth
 Dockyard launched 20.8.36—*Aurora*. Scotts launched 9.8.34—*Galatea*.

HMS Kenya (Cruiser)

Displacement: 8000 tons standard.
Dimensions: length 538ft (163·5m) pp, 555½ft (168·5m) oa; beam
 62ft (19m).
Draught: 16½ft (5m).
Propulsion: Geared turbines. 4 shafts. SHP 72500.
Speed: 33 knots.
Armament: Twelve 6in (152mm) guns (4×3). Eight 4in (102mm)
 A/A (4×2). Nine 2pdr A/A guns (2×4 and 1×1). Six 21in (533mm)
 torpedoes (2×3) AWTT.
Protection: Main belt 3¼in (82mm). Deck and Turrets 2in (51mm).
 DCT 4in (102mm).
Aircraft: Three.
Complement: 730.
Builders: John Brown launched 18.8.39.

HMS Neptune (Cruiser)

Displacement: 7175 tons standard.
Dimensions: length 530ft (161m) pp, 554½ft (168m) oa; beam 55¼ft
 (16·8m).
Draught: 16ft (4·9m).
Propulsion: Geared turbines. 4 shafts. SHP 72000.
Speed: 32½ knots.
Armament: Eight 6in (152mm) guns (4×2). Eight 4in (102mm) A/A

guns (4 × 2). Eight 2pdr A/A (2 × 4). Eight 21in (533mm) torpedoes (2 × 4) AWTT.

Protection: Main belt 2–4in (51–102mm). Deck 2in (51mm). Turrets and DCT 1in (25mm).

Aircraft: One

Complement: 550.

Builders: Portsmouth Dockyard launched 31.1.33.

HMS Hermione (Cruiser)

Displacement: 5450 tons standard.

Dimensions: length 485ft (148m) pp, 512ft (155m) oa; beam 50½ft (15.4m).

Draught: 14ft (4.3m).

Propulsion: Geared turbines. 4 shafts. SHP 62000.

Speed: 33 knots.

Armament: Ten 5.25in (133mm) DP guns (5 × 2). Eight 2pdr A/A guns (2 × 4). Six 21in (533mm) torpedoes (2 × 3) AWTT.

Protection: Main belt 2–3in (51–76mm). Deck ½–2in (13–51mm). Turrets 1–2in (25–51mm). DCT 1in (25mm).

Complement: 550.

Builders: Stephen launched 18.5.39.

HMS Inglefield (Destroyer—flotilla leader)

Displacement: 1530 tons.

Dimensions: length 326ft (98.8m) pp, 337ft (102.2m) oa; beam 34ft (10.3m).

Draught: 9ft (2.7m).

Propulsion: Geared turbines. 2 shafts. SHP 38000.

Speed: 36 knots.

Armament: Five 4.7in (119mm) DP guns (5 × 1). Ten 21in (533mm) torpdoes (2 × 5) AWTT.

Complement: 175.

Builder: Cammell Laird launched 15.10.36.

HMS Intrepid and Icarus (Destroyers)

Displacement: 1370 tons

Dimensions: length 321ft (94.6m) pp, 323ft (98m) oa; beam 32¼ft (9.8m).

Draught: 8½ft (2.6m).

Propulsion: Geared turbines. 2 shafts. SHP 34000.

Speed: 36 knots.

Armament: Four 4.7in (119mm) DP guns (4 × 1). Ten 21in (533mm) torpedoes (2 × 5) AWTT.

Complement: 145.

Builders: White launched 17.12.36—*Intrepid.* John Brown launched 26.11.36—*Icarus.*

HMS Echo and Electra (Destroyers)

Displacement: 1375 tons standard.
Dimensions: length 318¼ft (96·5m) pp, 329ft (100m) oa; beam 33¼ft (10m).
Draught: 8½ft (2·6m).
Propulsion: Geared turbines. 2 shafts. SHP 36000.
Speed: 35½ knots.
Armament: Four 4·7in (119mm) DP guns (4× 1). Eight 21in (533mm) torpedoes (2× 4) AWTT.
Builders: Denny Brothers launched 16.2.34—*Echo.* Hawthorn Leslie launched 15.2.34—*Electra.*

HMS Anthony, Achates, Antelope, Active and Hesperus*
(Destroyers)

Displacement: 1350 tons standard.
Dimensions: length 312ft (95m) pp, 323ft (98m) oa; beam 32¼ft (10·5m).
Draught: 8½ft (2·6m).
Propulsion: Geared turbines. 2 shafts. SHP 34000.
Speed: 35 knots.
Armament: Four 4·7in (119mm) guns (4× 1). Two 2pdr A/A guns (2× 1). Eight 21in (533mm) torpedoes (2× 4) AWTT.
Complement: 138.
Builders: Scotts launched 24.4.29—*Anthony.* J. Brown launched 4.10.29 —*Achates.* Hawthorn Leslie 27.7.29—*Antelope.* Hawthorn Leslie 9.7.29—*Active.* Thornycroft launched 1.8.39—*Hesperus.*

HMS Jupiter (Destroyer)

Displacement: 1690 tons standard.
Dimensions: length 339½ft (103m) pp, 356½ft (108m) oa; beam 35¾ft (10·8m).
Draught: 9ft (2·7m).
Propulsion: Geared turbines. 2 shafts. SHP 40000.
Speed: 36 knots.
Armament: Six 4·7in (119mm) guns (3× 2). Four 2pdr A/A guns (1× 4). Ten 21in (533mm) torpedoes (2× 5) AWTT.
Complement: 183.
Builders: Yarrow Ltd launched 27.10.38.

HMCS Assiniboine (Destroyer)

Displacement: 1390 tons standard.

---

* ex *Brazillian*

83

Dimensions: length 317¾ft (96·4m) pp, 329ft (100m) oa; beam 33ft (10m).
Draught: 8¾ft (2·4m).
Speed: 35½ knots.
Propulsion: Geared turbines. 2 shafts. SHP 36000.
Armament: Four 4·7in (119mm) guns (4×1). Two 2 pdr A/A guns (2×1). Eight 21in (533mm) torpedoes (2×4) AWTT.
Complement: 175.
Builders: Whites launched 29.10.31.

HMCS Saguenay (Destroyer)
Displacement: 1337 tons standard.
Dimensions: length 309ft (93·7m) pp, 321¼ft (97·5m) oa; beam 32¾ft (9·8m).
Draught: 8½ft (2·3m).
Speed: 34 knots.
Propulsion: Geared turbines. 2 shafts. SHP 32000.
Armament: Four 4·7in (119mm) guns (4×1). Two 2pdr A/A guns (2×1). Eight 21in (533mm) torpedoes (2×4) AWTT.
Complement: 138.
Builders: Thornycroft launched 11.7.30.

HMCS Columbia (Destroyer)
Displacement: 1060 tons standard.
Dimensions: length 309ft (93·7m) pp. 314¼ft (95m) oa; beam 30½ft (9·3m).
Draught: 8½ft (2·5m).
Propulsion: Geared turbines. 2 shafts. SHP 27000.
Speed: 35 knots.
Armament: Three 4in (102mm) guns (3×1). One 3in (76mm) A/A. Four 20mm A/A (4×1). Three 21in (533mm) torpedoes (1×3) AWTT. One Hedgehog A/S weapon.
Complement: 146.
Builders: Newport News USA launched 4.7.18.

HMS Faulknor (Destroyer—flotilla leader)
Displacement: 1475 tons standard.
Dimensions: length 332ft (101m) pp, 343ft (104m) oa; beam 33¾ft (10m).
Draught: 8¾ft (2·6m).
Propulsion: Geared turbines. 2 shafts. SHP 38000.
Speed: 36 knots.
Armament: Five 4·7in (119mm) guns (5×1). Eight 21in (533mm) torpedoes (2×4) AWTT.

Complement: 175.
Builders: Yarrow Ltd launched 12.6.34.

HMS Foresight, Forester, Foxhound and Fury (Destroyers)
Displacement: 1375 tons.
Dimensions: length 318¼ft (96·5m) pp, 329ft (99·8m) oa; beam 33¼ft (10m).
Draught: 8½ft (2·6m).
Propulsion: Geared turbines. 2 shafts. SHP 36000.
Speed: 35½ knots.
Armament: Four 4·7in (119mm) guns (4 × 1). Eight 21in (533mm) torpedoes (2 × 4) AWTT.
Builders: Cammell Laird launched 29.6.34—*Foresight*. Whites launched 28.6.34—*Forester*. J. Brown launched 12.10.34—*Foxhound*. Whites launched 10.9.34—*Fury*.

HMS Lance and Legion (Destroyers)
Displacement: 1920 tons standard.
Dimensions: length 345½ft (105m) pp, 362½ft (110m) oa; beam 36¾ft (11·2m).
Draught: 10ft (3m).
Propulsion: Geared turbines. 2 shafts. SHP 48000.
Speed: 36 knots.
Armament: Eight 4in (102mm) A/A guns (4 × 2). Four 2pdr A/A guns (1 × 4). Two 20mm A/A guns (2 × 1). Eight 21in (533mm) torpedoes (2 × 4) AWTT.
Complement: 226.
Builders: Yarrow Ltd launched 28.11.40—*Lance*. Hawthorn Leslie launched 26.12.39—*Legion*.

HMS Nestor and Polish Piorun (Destroyers)
Displacement: 1690 tons standard.
Dimensions: length 339½ft (103m) pp, 356½ft (108m) oa; beam 35¾ft (11m).
Draught: 9ft (2·7m).
Propulsion: Geared turbines. 2 shafts. SHP 40000.
Speed: 36 knots.
Armament: Six 4·7in (119mm) guns (3 × 2). Four 2pdr A/A guns (1 × 4). Two 20mm A/A guns (2 × 1). Ten 21in (533mm) torpedoes (2 × 5) AWTT.
Complement: 183.
Builders: Fairfield launched 9.7.40—*Nestor*. J. Brown launched 7.5.40—*Piorun*.

HMS Cossack, Maori, Zulu, Sikh, Somali, Mashona, Tartar and Punjabi (Tribal class destroyers)
Displacement: 1870 tons standard.
Dimensions: length 355½ft (108m) pp, 377½ft (114·6m) oa; beam 36½ft (11·1m).
Draught: 9ft (2·7m).
Propulsion: Geared turbines. 2 shafts. SHP 44000.
Speed: 36 knots.
Armament: Eight 4·7in (119mm) guns (4×2). Four 2pdr A/A guns (1×4). Four 21in (533mm) torpedoes (1×4) AWTT.
Complement: Cossack, Somali, Tartar 219, remainder 190.
Builders: Vickers Armstrong launched 8.6.37 and 3.9.37—*Cossack* and *Mashona*. Fairfield launched 7.7.37—*Maori*. Stephen launched 17.2.37 and 23.9.37—*Sikh* and *Zulu*. Swan Hunter launched 24.8.37 and 21.10.37—*Somali* and *Tartar*. Scotts launched 18.12.37—*Punjabi*.

HMS Windsor (Destroyer)
Displacement: 1100 tons standard.
Dimensions: length 300ft (91m) pp, 312ft (95m) oa; beam 29½ft (9m).
Draught: 10¾ft (3·3m).
Propulsion: Geared turbines. 2 shafts. SHP 27000.
Speed: 34 knots.
Armament: Three 4·7in (119mm) guns (3×1). One 3in (76mm) A/A gun. Two 2pdr A/A guns (2×1). Four 20mm A/A guns (4×1). Three 21in (533mm) torpedoes (1×3) AWTT.
Complement: 125.
Builders: Scotts launched 21.6.18.

APPENDIX III

Ship's Data (German)

Battleship Bismarck (Captain Ernst Lindemann)
Displacement: 41700 tons standard, 50900 tons full load.
Dimensions: length 823¼ft (251m) pp, 790½ft (241m) wl; beam 118ft 1in (36m).
Draught: 33½ft (10·2m) forward, 28½ft (8·7m) aft.
Propulsion: 12 Wagner high pressure boilers operating at 870lb/in² (60·7kg/cm²) at a temperature of 842°F (450°C) in two boiler rooms

supplying three sets of turbines driving 3 shafts developing 138000 SHP.

Speed: 30·8 knots on trials, designed 29½ knots.

Armament: Eight 15in (381mm) guns (4 × 2). Twelve 5·9in (150mm) guns (6 × 2) three each side. Sixteen 4·1in (105mm) A/A guns (8 × 2) four each side. Sixteen 37mm A/A guns (8 × 2). Sixteen 20mm A/A guns (16 × 1).

Protection: Main belt 12·5in (320mm) from just forward of foremost turret to just abaft the after one. It extended from the upper deck to 6½ft (2m) below the full load waterline. The upper deck was made of 2in (50mm) special steel below which was the armoured deck 4in (102mm) thick covering four-fifths of the ship's length and sloping at the sides to meet the lower edge of the main belt. The thickness of the sloping portion was increased to 4¾in (120mm). Interior antitorpedo compartments were made of a special soft tensile steel known as Wotan-weich–Material.

Aircraft: Six Arado type 196.

Radio/Radar: Two Direction Finding sets and one search radar set.

Complement: 2200 with Admiral's staff.

Builders: Blohm und Voss, Hamburg, launched 14.2.39.

Cruiser Prinz Eugen (Captain Helmuth Brinkmann)

Displacement: 16230 tons standard, 18400 tons full load.

Dimensions: Length 655ft (199·7m) wl; beam 71ft (21·6m).

Propulsion: Combined Diesel and Geared steam turbines. 4 shafts.

Speed: 32 knots.

Armament: Eight 8in (203mm) guns (4 × 2). Twelve 4·1in (105mm) A/A guns (6 × 2). Twelve 37mm A/A guns (6 × 2). Twelve 21in (533mm) torpedoes (4 × 3).

Protection: Main belt 5in (127mm), bridge 2in (51mm).

Aircraft: Four and one catapult.

Builders: Deschimag & Co—Germania.

Note on German Radar

In September 1935 Admiral Raeder was shown an experimental type of radar fitted in the trials ship *Welle* and early in 1939 the German navy took delivery of its first Freya radar set which is said to have had a range of 75 miles. It was given the cover name of Dezimeter Telegraphie or D.T.Geräte, but interest seems to have been focussed on the development of a tactical set and the *Graf Spee* was equipped with a short range set known as Seetakt, which employed 375 megacycles and had a range of 9 miles. According to Herr Brennecke there is some doubt regarding whether or not the *Bismarck* was fitted with a radar set, although amongst the technical details one Radio warning set is included and 'a matress type antenna 2 × 6 metres on the foreside of the D.T. Geräte was observed', which would appear to indicate that she was so equipped.

Aircraft Data

Swordfish
Nos 810 and 818 squadrons—HMS *Ark Royal*.
Nos 820 and 825 squadrons—HMS *Victorious*.
825 Squadron Leader—Lieutenant-Commander Eugene Esmonde RN.
818 Squadron Leader—Lieutenant-Commander T. P. Coode RN.
Carrier-borne, torpedo-spotter-reconnaissance aircraft.
Crew—Three for reconnaissance, two for torpedo attack.
Metal structure, fabric covered.
Manufactured by Fairey Aviation Company, Hayes, Middlesex, sub-
contractors Blackburn Aircraft Ltd, Brough.
Power plant: one 690hp Bristol Pegasus III M3 or 750hp Pegasus XXX.
Dimensions: Span 45ft 6in (folded 17ft 3in), length 36ft 4in, height
12ft 10in, wing area 607 square feet, weight—light, 5200lb, loaded
9250lb.
Performance: Maximum speed 139mph at 4750ft, cruising 104/129mph
at 5000ft. Range 546 miles with one 1610lb torpedo.

Fulmar
No 800Z Squadron onboard HMS *Victorious* comprised six of these
aircraft. Due to excellent night reconnaissance by them the Swordfish
aircraft were able to attack the *Bismarck* on the night of May 24/25.
Two-seater carrier-borne fighter. All metal stressed skin construction.
Manufactured by Fairey Aviation Company.
Power plant: one 1080hp Rolls-Royce Merlin VIII.
Dimensions: span 46ft 4½in, length 40ft 3in, height 14ft, wing area
342 square feet, weight loaded 9800lb.
Performance: Maximum speed 280mph, cruising 235mph, rate of
climb 1200ft per minute, range 800 miles, ceiling 26000ft.
Armament: Eight fixed Browning guns some with single Vickers K
gun in rear cockpit.
Entered service in June 1940.

Torpedoes Fired at Bismarck

Ship	Time of Attack	No of Torpedoes Fired (Jettisoned)	Hits	Possible Hits
Victorious	2400/25	8 (1)	1	—
Ark Royal	1550/26 on HMS Sheffield	—	—	—
	2100/26	13 (2)	2	1
	1016/27	Nil (15)	—	—
Cossack	0140/27	3	1	—
	0335/27	1	—	—
Maori	0137/27	2	1	—
	0656/27	2	—	—
Zulu	0121/27	4	—	—
Sikh	0128/27	4	—	1
Rodney	During the action on May 27	12	1	—
Norfolk	ditto	8	—	1
Dorsetshire	1025/27	3	2	1

Total number fired 71
expended 92

Hits	Possible Hits
8	4

Ammunition Expended During Final Action Against Bismarck, May 27, 1941

Ship	16in (41cm)	14in (35·6cm)	8in (20·3cm)	6in (15·2cm)	5·25in (13·3cm)
King George V	—	339	—	—	660
Rodney	380	—	—	716	—
Norfolk	—	—	527	—	—
Dorsetshire	—	—	254	—	—
Total	380	339	781	716	660

APPENDIX VII

Honours and Awards

In the London Gazette of October 14, 1941, it was announced that HM the King had given orders for the following appointments and awards for distinguished services 'in the masterly and determined action in which the *Bismarck* was destroyed':

To Admiral Sir John Tovey KCB, DSO, Commander-in-Chief, Home Fleet a KBE.

To Rear-Admiral (then Captain) F. G. H. Dalrymple-Hamilton, HMS *Rodney*, and Captain W. R. Patterson CVO, RN, HMS *King George V*, a CB.

To Rear-Admiral W. F. Wake-Walker CB, Captain H. C. Bovell R,N HMS *Victorious*, Commodore 1st Class E. J. P. Brind, Chief of Staff to the C-in-C, Home Fleet, and Captain L. E. H. Maund RN, HMS *Ark Royal* a CBE.

Rear-Admiral (then Captain) P. L. Vian a Second Bar to the DSO.

Captain J. C. Leach MVO, RN, HMS *Prince of Wales* and a further ten officers were awarded a DSO, nineteen were awarded a DSC and six received an OBE. Twenty-seven ratings received the DSM, and one a BEM.

Awards to officers and men of the Fleet Air Arm for their part in the operation included three DSO's, eleven DSC's and five DSM's.

The Commanding Officer of the Sunderland aircraft which shadowed the *Bismarck* on May 23 and the pilot of the Catalina aircraft which relocated her on May 26 received the DFC.

Vice-Admiral L. E. Holland CB, Captain R. Kerr CBE, RN and Lieutenant-Commander E. H. F. Moultrie of HMS *Hood* received a posthumous mention in despatches, together with 33 other officers and men of the ill-fated ship.

Bibliography

Bismarck (The Sinking of) Supplement to the London Gazette No 38098, Admiral Sir John Tovey's despatch on the action.

The War At Sea Volume 1 by Captain S. W. Roskill RN—HMSO.

The History of the Second World War Vol. 2, Editor in Chief Sir Basil Liddell Hart—Purnell and Sons.

Schlachtschiff BISMARCK by Jochen Brennecke—US Naval Institute and Koehlers Verlagsgesellschaft Herford 1960.

The Bismarck Episode by Captain Russell Grenfell RN—Faber & Faber, 1948.

The Cruise of the Bismarck by Francis McMurtrie—Hutchinson & Co.

The Führer Naval Conferences—HMSO.

Struggle for the Sea by Grand Admiral Erich Raeder—Wm Kimber.

Sea Warfare 1939–45 by Vice-Admiral F. Rüge—Cassell.

The German Navy in World War II by Edward P. von der Porten—Arthur Barker, 1970.

The Mighty Hood by Ernle Bradford—Hodder & Stoughton 1959.

Schlachtschiff und Schlachtkreuzer by Siegfried Breyer 1905–1970.

British Battleships by Oscar Parkes.

Exploits and End of the Battleship Bismarck by Captain Gerhard Bidlingmaier—US Naval Institute Proceedings July 1958.

Index

Rank abbreviations:
A. of F., Admiral of the Fleet; Ad., Admiral; V.-Ad., Vice-Admiral; R.-Ad., Rear-Admiral; Comdre., Commodore; Capt., Captain; Cdr., Commander; Lt.-Cdr., Lieutenant-Commander; A.C.M., Air Chief Marshal; F/O, Flying Officer.